ACCESSING SUPERNATURAL GRACE

Letting the Holy Spirit Lead You in the Prayer Closet

Bo Salisbury

Visit Kingdom Culture International at https://www.kingdomculture.life

Accessing Supernatural Grace: Letting the Holy Spirit Lead You in the Prayer Closet by *Bo Salisbury*

Cover design by Christopher Negron

Published by *Kingdom Culture Media*

Originally published as **Accessing Supernatural Grace: Kingdom-focused Prayer** *February 2016*

ISBN 978-1717430106   ISBN 1717430104

First printing April 2018

23 24 22 21 20 19 18

12 11 10 9 8 7 6 5 4

Printed in the United States of America

Table of Contents

Preface

At the age of twelve I had a life-altering experience with the Lord that forever changed my perspective and pursuit of Jesus Christ in my life. Although I had been raised in a Christian home and attended church ever since I came out of the womb, I had been under a demonic assault that aimed to hinder my spiritual calling from coming forth and ultimately, to take my very life. For two years I lived under intense depression and loneliness, driven by fears that kept me bound up on the inside, unable to express myself in normal ways.

Looking out my bedroom window in the summer of 1984, I resolved to take my life. So I turned around to get the gun from my father's closet but to my surprise, the Lord himself was standing between me and the bedroom door! As soon as I saw him in his glorious light I fell to the floor, weeping in his presence. What followed was a brief conversation that addressed the warfare that had been going on in my mind. Jesus told me to give my life to him, to which I replied "if life is going to be like this, I don't want to live!" His response still rings in my ears: "give your life to me and I will make something great out of it!"

I have never seen love so pure or truth so intense as I did that day when I looked into his eyes! After he said this, all I could do was weep and say, "Yes! Yes!" Immediately after I said that, he put his right hand on my shoulder and the oppression I had carried for the previous two years was instantly broken! My heart was flooded with his love and I experienced a freedom I had never known before! My world was forever changed. It was as if my life went from black and white to Ultra HD color in an instant!!

"Give your life to me and I will make something great out of it!"

As you can probably imagine, this experience had a tremendous effect on my personal prayer life. Reading the Word took on new meaning after I had met the Word Himself! Worship became more intimate after having seen with my own eyes just how much he loved me! Talking to God went to another level after hearing His voice with my own two ears!! Although I haven't seen Jesus with my own eyes since this experience, He has become even more real to me throughout the years. In response to my pursuit of Him, God has increasingly revealed more of His nature and ability to me by virtue of His amazing grace!

It is my sincere desire that your relationship with the Lord will soar to new heights as you pursue His Kingdom and welcome the grace that is released in your life because of your pursuit of Him! I pray that God will use this book to speak to your heart in ways that will liberate you from every hindrance to knowing Him more! I pray that the freshness of the Spirit will be poured out like a torrential downpour on your life in this season! May the Lord enlighten you to that which you may be oblivious to so you can access what He wants to give you: an abundant supply of His grace! I decree that you will receive the very grace you need to fulfill every dream He has put in your heart to accomplish for His glory!!

Bo Salisbury

Grace Life International

INTRODUCTION

The Gracious Kingdom

*"But seek first his kingdom and his
righteousness, and all these things will be
given to you as well."* **Matthew 6:33**

There's a play in the game of football called the "Hail Mary." When the losing team has just enough time for one last desperation play, the coach usually calls for the "Hail Mary." The quarterback heaves the ball down the field with the wild hope that somehow, someway, one of his teammates will catch the ball in the end zone to win the game. Given the high degree of difficulty, less than 1% of "Hail Mary" plays are successful.

This play has a Catholic connotation to prayers that are made to Mary that obviously never get answered because she's dead. But it also reveals an attitude with prayer in general, that prayer is nothing more than a hope that we can catch God in a good enough mood to grant our requests! With this mindset we supposedly have to twist His holy arm in heaven to give us what we want!!

Truth is, this philosophy affects the prayers of believers today who have yet to grasp the revelation that our loving heavenly Father desires to give us everything we need. Without a revelation of His will, there can be no faith for what He wants to give us. And without faith fueling our prayers, they are at best only hope-based. The problem with this equation is that God does not respond to hope, He only responds to our faith.

One reason believers sometimes lack faith for God to answer their prayers is because they don't feel like they measure up. They don't think they deserve God's blessings based on their shortcomings. This belief reveals the need to understand God's grace more accurately. God's grace is not released in our lives based on our goodness, but on His alone. No amount of good behavior qualifies us for answered prayer. The only thing that qualifies us is our faith in the finished work of Christ. According to **Romans 5:2**, faith is the only thing that gives us access to His grace.

The Abundance of Grace

When believers begin to pray according to faith that is birthed out a revelation of God's love, they begin to see results. And with results, the mindset that views prayer as nothing more than a "Hail Mary" football play begins to dissipate. But with a further revelation of the Kingdom of God, which will bring about yet another paradigm shift, there will be another level of freedom and fulfilment in their prayer lives. It's one thing for someone to pray with their own needs in mind. But it's another thing to pray with the desires of the King in mind.

God's grace is not released in our lives based on our goodness, but on His alone

As **Matthew 6:33** reveals, if our pursuit is first and foremost the expansion of God's Kingdom in and through our lives, God will see to it that every resource we need will be supplied to us! When our motive isn't just to satisfy our personal desires but to see our lives used in service for the King, we prove to God that He can trust us with an abundance of His grace and blessings.

For example, when your prayers shift from getting your needs met to being able to meet the needs of others, you are positioning yourself for abundant financial blessings. When your motive shifts from personal fulfilment to the freedom to fulfill your heavenly calling, get ready for a release of God's grace in your life you've never seen! If you want to access supernatural grace, you must have faith. But if you want to access the "abundance of grace" that **Romans 5:17** refers to, you must use your faith for the expansion of God's kingdom, not just your own needs.

There is yet another level of effectiveness in prayer where we stop asking God for things and we begin speaking them into existence. There comes a point where we need to stop asking God to do for us what He has already told us to do for ourselves. We need to mature in our faith to the place where we "speak those things that aren't as if they were" so they will be! Remember that we were created in His image and were given authority on the earth to govern our world just like He rules the heavens. God expects us to walk in dominion because He has given us the authority to do so through the faith in our hearts and the words of our mouths.

We need to mature in our faith to the place where we "speak those things that aren't as if they were" so they will be!

The kingdom of God beckons those who will increasingly relinquish control of their lives for a greater purpose, submitting to the desires of the King. Surrendering what is required by Him grants access to what one cannot earn and does not deserve. Placing priority on the culture of heaven in one's life ensures that God will supply every resource that is necessary to carry out one's earthly assignment. That's because God can trust the one who entrusts everything to Him and will therefore give whatever is needed to the one who gives Him his all.

God never promised to give us what we ask of Him. Our requests need to agree with heaven to move His heart on our behalf. However, if our petitions are connected to our Kingdom assignment, then He promised to give us anything we need! Without a Kingdom perspective we tend to focus on our felt needs and have the tendency to lean on our own righteousness as the basis for asking God to meet them. But God doesn't answer prayer based on our goodness. He responds to faith that is connected to Kingdom purpose. Part of that Kingdom purpose is to meet our personal needs because our King is also our Father. But there is a greater spiritual purpose at stake than food in our belly and a roof over our head, that is, if we are focused on His Kingdom.

CHAPTER ONE

Where Does the Time Go?

"My times are in your hands." **Psalm 31:15**

As each New Year approaches, I'm reminded that time slows down for no one. Our days on earth are so very valuable, not only to our individual lives but for eternity itself. God placed each one of us here in this season, for a specific reason. In order to achieve true fulfillment in life, we need to discover our purpose, develop our giftedness, delight to do God's perfect will and determine to allow the grace of God to continuously unfold in our lives. That way, we will never stop learning, changing or ministering to others what God has invested in us. Easier said than done, but it all boils down to this: every day is an opportunity to know Him more and for Him to make Himself known through you.

No amount of effort can change a single thing in the past, but your future awaits the decisions you will make in response to the revelation of His will, even in the face of contrary circumstances that often demand your attention. Forgive my dry humor, but today truly is the first day of the rest of your life! If you could see your life from God's perspective, you would know the absolute importance of each day, not only for your sake but for those around you. As James 4:14 puts it, "What is your life? You are a mist that appears for a little while and then vanishes." Compared to eternity, 80 years is a drop in a bucket!

Every day is an opportunity to know Him more and for Him to make Himself known through you

---

Sometimes I wish I could go back in time and reverse a number of decisions I've made over the years. And if I was a betting man, I would put money on the premonition that I am not alone on this one! If you knew back then what you know right now, what would you have done differently? Probably a whole lot, right?

Although living in the land of regret won't do you any good, accessing the wisdom of God based on your past mistakes is invaluable to making better decisions in the future. They say "hindsight is 20/20" but unfortunately not everyone learns from past mistakes, even when they are fully aware of them. Truthfully, our own stubbornness leads us to repeat dysfunctional patterns because we tend to trust in our wisdom more than His.

Let me encourage you to embrace this season with a bulldog tenacity to make the most of each day. As the Israelites of old made a point to gather manna each day, make it your goal to prioritize what is really important in your life: hearing and responding to the voice of God. Without a revelation of His will for your life, you are left wondering what your purpose is and end up wandering from that purpose.

Without a clear sense of direction, the winds of circumstance will dictate the course of your life. You don't have to be a victim of circumstance. You can take charge of your life by surrendering it to Him today! A paradox worth living for, if you ask me.

Father Knows Best

You might be saying to yourself right now: "but I have surrendered my life to Him and I still feel helpless in my situation!" Maybe you're not sure what your purpose is or maybe you do but don't know how to go about fulfilling it. If that's you, understand that you're not alone. Many believers today put on their Sunday suits and smiles and present the image that everything is hunky-dory while their insides are crying out for something more. They are aware that something is missing, that they are somehow not living up to their potential.

I must say that I have been in this very position a number of times in my life, the last of which wasn't that long ago. Times of internal frustration with external circumstances are often the result of depending on our own wisdom instead of accessing His. When we become complacent in gathering daily manna in our lives, this is indicative of our tendency to "lean on our own understanding" instead of trusting our daily lives to the leading of His Spirit. We somehow think we know how to run our lives better than He does. Ludicrous, isn't it?

Many believers today put on their Sunday suits and smiles and present the image that everything

is hunky-dory while their insides are crying out
for something more

Surrendering your life to Christ should not be a one-time experience; it should be a continual process of acknowledging your need for Him more than your next breath. Jesus demonstrated this for us through his lifestyle of dependence on the voice of the Father and the empowerment of the Spirit. When we read about the miracles Jesus performed it's easy to assume that they were done because he was God in the flesh. But Jesus never did anything supernatural until he received the empowerment of the Spirit. Even after the Spirit "descended like a dove upon him" he didn't rush off to start his world-shaking ministry. He got alone with God for 40 days.

Jesus the Hulk?

Jesus wasn't a first century version of the Incredible Hulk, half God and half man. He was 100% Son of God and 100% Son of man. As the Son of God He was the Living Word and the Bread from heaven, but as the Son of man he depended on the voice of the Father for identity, instruction and direction. Jesus refused to teach anything that he didn't first hear his Father say. (**John 7:16**) And he refused to do anything that he didn't first see his Father do. (**John 5:19**) He didn't just go about randomly teaching people what he decided from day to day and healing people when he was in a good mood.

His message and his mission came from heaven and he was responsible enough to stop and listen for orders from headquarters. The moment he sensed the strength of his spirit waning after expending himself through sacrificial ministry, he found a way to get alone with God for refreshment and to re-orient himself for the next mini-mission along his journey to fulfill his ultimate mission on the cross.

Jesus consistently spent time with the Father in prayer, which resulted in an incredibly accurate and powerful ministry. Sometimes it was early in the morning, sometimes late at night. He would often go up a mountain to pray. The place and time weren't as important as the priority he placed upon it. He connected with the Father on a consistent basis because the temptations that accompanied his physical body and soul demanded that he draw strength and wisdom from heaven, not only to overcome temptation but to fulfill God's will. His goal wasn't simply to avoid the pitfalls of sin; it was to fulfill all righteousness. And that he did on a tree.

Immediately after Jesus spent 40 days and nights connecting with God in the desert, the devil tempted him to function as the Son of God by turning stones into sandwiches. (OK, I modified that a little) The temptation was to use his spiritual identity as the Son of God to feed his flesh. Not only did Jesus refuse to do this, but he silenced the voice of the enemy by quoting this Scripture: "Man does not live on bread alone, but on every word that comes from the mouth of God." (**Matthew 4:4**)

Jesus Didn't Have Identity Issues

Jesus didn't deny his identity as the Son of God with this statement. Nor did he deny the fact that he was ready to throw down at the Jerusalem Golden Corral buffet! What he revealed was that his life's decisions weren't dictated merely by external circumstances, but by an ever-proceeding Word from the Father. As our natural bodies depend on a consistent intake of nutrients in order to function properly, so the health of our spirits depends on receiving His Word into our hearts and allowing the Spirit to apply it to our lives consistently.

This verse is actually a direct reference to the Israelites gathering the manna that God supplied for them in the desert. The fact that He gave them exactly what they needed every day is a good indication that He wants to do the same for you today. If you are a born again believer, then the Spirit of Christ lives inside of you and has been commissioned to reveal Jesus to you. He is poised to reveal the will of the Father to you. He is able to show you who you are in Christ and who He is in you. He can give you the strength and wisdom not only to overcome your temptations but to fulfill your purpose too!

The only way the Holy Spirit can fulfill His purpose in your life is IF you allow Him to help you fulfill your purpose! This involves you putting your faith in God's ability to do what only He can do as well as asking for His wisdom to do what you need to do. It's a partnership made in heaven. You and God are a team. And together you can accomplish anything He puts into your heart to do!

The only way the Holy Spirit can fulfill His purpose in your life is IF you allow Him to help you fulfill your purpose!

Think of the Word of God as your source of spiritual nutrition. It gives you the strength to survive and the sustenance to thrive, the wisdom to achieve and the ability to believe that anything is possible! D.L. Moody once said that "the Scriptures were not given to increase our knowledge but to change our lives." So true! When the knowledge of the Word you obtained yesterday becomes more important than the life the Word can give you today, you are essentially sacrificing the wisdom of God on the altar of your own agenda.

His ways are higher than ours and His thoughts far exceed our wildest imaginations. Place a premium on His will by making each day just a little more important than the one before. After all, you are a day closer to eternity than you were yesterday. Time is precious and so is His voice. Ask the Lord to make you sensitive to hear, ready to learn, willing to change, determined to obey and hungry for more of Him.

If Jesus Christ, who is the very Word of God Himself, chose to lay aside his deity and take upon himself human flesh like you and I, this is proof enough that he has made tremendous effort to bridge the gap between your life and your spiritual purpose. If it was necessary for Jesus to maintain his spirit through prayer, then I think it is extremely self-righteous for us to think that we can go about our lives any other way than he modeled for us: a life in love with Him! He embraced his cross for us. We should do the same for Him. The only way to obtain true life is through the death of our fleshly desire to maintain control in our lives. Surrender your all, die daily and discover what a joy it is to allow His life to flow through you.

CHAPTER TWO

Our Invitation to Know Him

"We proclaim to you what we have seen and heard, so that you also may have fellowship with us. And our fellowship is with the Father and with his Son, Jesus Christ." **I John 1:3**

In Christian circles, we throw the phrase "relationship with God" out there like everyone knows what that means, when in reality it means different things to different people. I find that people usually view their relationship with God through the rose-colored glasses of their Christian experience and through traditions they learned from people who told them what that should look like. But how does the Word of God describe our relationship with Him?

In **Matthew 15**, the Pharisees and teachers of the law asked Jesus a question that revealed the basis for their relationship with God. They asked him why his disciples did not follow the tradition of the elders. Jesus discretely answered their question with another question: *"And why do you break the command of God for the sake of your tradition?"* This is a very interesting dialogue between Jesus and the Pharisees because it exposes the hypocrisy in the hearts of people who were given the Law to guide them into a true relationship with God, and yet they placed greater importance upon what other people said and did (the tradition of the elders) than what God actually said Himself.

Jesus then gave an example of what the Law told them to do and contrasted it with what they actually practiced through their tradition, exposing the rationale that supported their "relationship with God." And to top it off, Jesus made a powerful statement that gives us a revelation of what happens when we blindly obey traditions of men while neglecting to follow the voice of God: we make the Word of God powerless in our lives!

Just think of the irony of such a statement! The very Word of God that created the universe is rendered powerless in our lives when we choose to make up our own rules instead of following His! When we try to shape the parameters of our relationship with God or allow others to define them for us, we isolate ourselves from the rules of engagement that God already established as the basis for our relationship with Him. And by doing so, we cut ourselves off from the blessing that is reserved for those who truly know God for themselves.

The very Word of God that created the universe is rendered powerless in our lives when we choose to make up our own rules instead of following His!

I think that we forget that it was God who invited us to be in relationship with Him, not the other way around! Therefore we don't have the right to tell God what our relationship with Him should look like. Either we relate with Him on His terms or we won't be able to truly know Him for ourselves.

Fortunately for us, this is not an all-or-nothing thing. In other words, we don't have to have it all figured out before we can know Him as our Father. We just need to accept His forgiveness and eternal life, and surrender our lives to Him to be born into His family. But to progress in our relationship with Him, we need to find out what He says in His Word and abide by it, thus invoking His blessing upon our lives, which is the fruit of a true relationship with God.

The Covenant of Grace

God has clearly defined the nature of our relationship with Him through the covenants He established with man from the beginning. A covenant contains the parameters for a committed relationship along with the responsibilities of each party. It also contains the purpose for relationship, the benefits for fulfilling the given responsibilities and the consequences for not following the rules of engagement. It's amazing to see God's unchanging desire to be in relationship with man through the covenants He established with men such as Adam, Noah, Abraham, Isaac, Jacob, Moses, David and finally Jesus.

Some theologians like to separate time as we know it into dispensations, which define how God related with man with a slightly different set of rules in each age. For instance, Adam lived in the Age of Innocence whereas Moses lived in the Age of the Law and today we live in the Age of Grace. Although there are distinct differences between these ages, the similarities are amazing! Check this out.

Adam, Noah, Abraham, Isaac, Jacob, Moses and David all received covenants from God which laid out the purpose for our relationship with God: to be more like God and to represent Him in the earth. All of these covenants made provision for man to know God by communicating with Him, worshiping Him, believing Him, obeying Him, and sharing Him with others, all of which still apply to us today!

According to **Galatians 3**, the same faith Abraham exercised in God and the same blessing that came upon his life are available to us, even in the New Covenant that Jesus established for us. If you track these covenants through Scripture, you will notice that they are not disconnected from each other. In fact, all of these covenants are progressive, building upon the previous one and being passed down from generation to generation (Abraham to Isaac to Jacob). The most misunderstood and misapplied covenant of all is perhaps the Old Covenant that was given to Moses.

The Law was an integral part of the progression in the chain of covenants that were designed to help facilitate the relationship between God and man. The Scripture reveals in **Galatians 3:19** that the Law was added BECAUSE of sin UNTIL the Seed (Christ) came to redeem us from the curse of the law. **Hebrews 9:10** also says that *"the external regulations of the law applied UNTIL the time of the new order"* that was introduced by Christ. From these two verses we understand that the Old Covenant (Law) served a specific purpose and for a specific time period.

The most misunderstood and misapplied covenant of all is perhaps the Old Covenant that was given to Moses

---

The law was added to condemn man's righteousness in the flesh and show man his need for God's righteousness. When Jesus came on the scene and revealed the righteousness of God by an internal faith as opposed to external works of the law, the law and all of its regulations were thus fulfilled by Christ Himself and done away with at the "cross road" of Calvary. (**Colossians 2:13-17, Ephesians 2:13-16**) The cross of Christ truly was a crossroad that presented a new and better path in pursuit of intimacy with God. It was the transition between two radically different covenants that paved the way for true relationship with God.

Difficulty Swallowing the Pill

The Pharisees struggled to receive this message of grace that Jesus began to proclaim in their generation. They were so accustomed to working for their salvation by adhering to external regulations of the law, that when they saw Jesus breaking some of their laws and traditions they couldn't get with the program.

Prior to receiving the Spirit of God at his water baptism, Jesus conformed to Jewish laws and traditions. But after that moment, he was committed to doing what his Father was doing and saying what his Father was saying. He placed greater emphasis on the Word of God than the tradition of the elders. In fact, he made a point to break the laws that were merely shadows of Himself. For instance, he broke the Sabbath laws because he is the Lord of the Sabbath. (**Matthew 12:8**) We now find our rest in him.

As Jesus began to teach his disciples how to have a personal relationship with God, he emphasized the importance of following the leading of the Holy Spirit, not the tradition of the elders. He emphasized hearing the voice of God and obeying God's Word. Although they couldn't fully comprehend what he was saying until the Holy Spirit took residence within their spirits, Jesus helped his followers focus on the motivations of the heart, not outward actions.

Jesus helped his followers focus on the motivations of the heart, not outward actions

For example, when speaking of the law in **Matthew 5,** Jesus said that "*he did not come to abolish the law, but to fulfill it.*" He then gave examples of murder and adultery, which are external sins. He said that we shouldn't even hate or lust, which are internal sins. He fulfilled these laws by perfecting them or by bringing them to a complete state where they were no longer written on tablets of stone, but in our hearts by the Holy Spirit. In this way, we could become *"living epistles, written by the Holy Spirit and read of all men!"* (**II Corinthians 3:3**)

However, when speaking of Christ extending the gospel of grace to the Gentiles, **Ephesians 2:15** says that Christ *"abolished the law and its regulations"* when he died on the cross. Now which is it? Did Christ come to abolish the law or not? **Matthew 5** says that he did NOT come to abolish the law but **Ephesians 2** says that he did. The answer to this question gives us a better understanding of what our relationship with God should look like. Both. How is that possible? Either he came to do away with the law or he didn't. Right?!?

Jesus, the Fulfillment of the Law

If you study the Word, you will find that there are numerous scriptures to confirm that he did, in fact, come to do away with the law. (**Colossians 2:13-17, Hebrews 7-10, Ephesians 2:13-16, Galatians 3:21-25**) **Matthew 5** is the only verse that says otherwise.

So to understand this apparent contradiction, you have to understand this: the Law served a definite purpose and was in effect for a definite time period. Its time period expired when Christ came on the scene. According to **Galatians 4**, *"in the fullness of time Christ was born under the law to redeem*

29

those who were under the law." He redeemed us from the curse of the law and introduced us to a better covenant, the gospel of grace.

The reason Jesus said that he didn't come to abolish it was to make the point that he wasn't introducing some totally new religion to humanity. He was cooperating with the Father to improve the relationship parameters between man and God through a new and living way, the new covenant of his blood and grace. *"The law came through Moses, but grace and truth came through Christ."*

He was saying that the law finds the fulfillment of its purpose in Christ. Commandments, such as 'not committing murder or adultery' aren't done away with, they are perfected by becoming matters of the heart. (don't hate or lust) But other commandments such as animal sacrifices and religious festivals, were done away with altogether because Jesus, the Lamb of God, became the final sacrifice and we should celebrate His new life every day!

All of the 613 Levitical laws were either done away with because Christ became the reality of the shadow they cast (**Colossians 2:17**) or improved upon to take on the nature of grace in our hearts (murder to hate, adultery to lust, etc.) After all, Jesus said that everything in the law had a purpose and would be fulfilled (**Matthew 5:17-18**). Of course, Jesus himself was the fulfillment of numerous prophecies in the Old Testament.

When it comes down to it, there is much to learn about our relationship with God and our responsibility to represent

Him in the earth by looking into the perfect law of liberty, allowing the Holy Spirit to illuminate to us the various types and shadows in the Old Testament Law. And as we respond to this revelation of Christ in the Scriptures of old, we become a doer of the Word that we become aware of. (**James 1:21-25**)

If you really want to know what your relationship with God should look like, don't use the Word to simply validate your Christian experience. Submit your experience to the wisdom of the Word and adjust it accordingly. And don't blindly carry out the tradition of your elders, taking somebody else's word for it. Hear it straight from the horse's mouth!

The same faith Abraham used to hear God's voice, believe His Word and obey the truth applies to all of us. And the same blessing upon his life is available for you and I because Christ has redeemed us from the curse of the law (**Galatians 3:13-14**).

> *Don't use the Word to simply validate your Christian experience. Submit your experience to the wisdom of the Word and adjust it accordingly*

But one huge advantage we have over Abraham is that we have the Spirit of God abiding on the inside! That's why we have a better covenant established on better promises. A true relationship with God gets better and better as we know Him more and more, and as He is made known through us every day. Thank God for His invitation to relationship with Him!

CHAPTER THREE

Say Grace, Say What?

*"May the grace of the Lord Jesus Christ, and
the love of God, and the fellowship of the
Holy Spirit be with you all."*

II Corinthians 13:14

Grace is possibly one of the most misused words in Christian vocabulary today. It's misused because it's misunderstood. And sadly enough, even though some have come to a degree of understanding of grace, it has been abused because people tend to push things to the extreme, twisting truth to their own destruction. While some are living a 'hyper grace' gospel, dismissing the consequences of sin, others are living a life of legalism, exalting rules and regulations above the power of Christ's finished work on the cross.

First of all, grace is not a prayer that we concoct prior to consuming food at the dinner table. That is a prayer of thanksgiving. Secondly, grace is not the equivalent of mercy, which is the withholding of punishment that we deserve.

Although this is an accurate definition of mercy, it is not true about grace. Thirdly, grace is often confused with forgiveness, which correlates with mercy. While mercy is about NOT RECEIVING punishment we deserve, forgiveness is about RECEIVING a total pardon for our sins that we don't deserve. Fourthly, being gracious in modern vernacular is synonymous with having a giving nature, which is only partially true about grace. While we know these meanings and use grace in our vocabulary quite frequently, they present a different image than God presents in His Word.

While some are living a 'hyper grace' gospel, dismissing the consequences of sin, others are living a life of legalism, exalting rules and regulations above the power of Christ's finished work on the cross

---

So what is grace? I'm glad you asked that question. We would do well to find out God's definition from His Word. But before we do that, let me share with you a very common definition of grace that you may have heard: the unmerited favor of God. I believe that this is accurate, and yet incomplete. Grace is without a doubt unmerited. There is nothing we can do to deserve it or earn it. And it certainly gives us an advantage (favor) over those who do not possess it. But this doesn't make us more loved by God or better than others who have not received God's grace. It just means there are benefits to receiving what God has provided for us.

So what does God have to say about grace? Although there are numerous scriptures we could look at on the subject, let's just look at a couple for now.

> *"For you know the <u>grace</u> of our Lord Jesus Christ, that though he was rich, yet for your sakes he became poor, so that you through his poverty might become rich."*

> **II Corinthians 8:9**

> *"Christ redeemed us from the curse of the law by becoming a curse for us, for it is written, 'cursed is everyone who is hung on a tree.' He redeemed us in order that the <u>blessing</u> given to Abraham might come to the Gentiles through Jesus Christ, so that by faith we might receive the promise of <u>the Spirit</u>."* **Galatians 3:13, 14**

This verse in **I Corinthians 8** is sandwiched between several other verses that deal with the subject of financial giving, which in this case was aimed at helping the poor Christians in Jerusalem that Paul was raising an offering for. This verse is sometimes skewed by preachers who push for a strong financial offering from believers who are told that their giving will make them rich. But a closer look at this passage reveals that we aren't supposed to give to get rich, we should give because we already are rich! Not financially but spiritually!!

Now before you jump on the bandwagon of the anti-prosperity, poverty-mentality bunch, understand that there are two sides to this coin! Because we are rich spiritually we have access to the wisdom and favor of God that can and will attract financial provision for everything we need if we follow His lead. What we receive in the spirit should eventually manifest in the material realm if we do our part. I think the difference lies in our definition of 'rich.' While the world may view being rich with having millions of dollars, God views it as having everything you need to fulfill your assignment.

Lovers of God are Givers

Jesus gave his life for us out of a sincere desire to see us receive his love. He wasn't selfishly motivated in his giving. He was thinking about us. This passage encourages us to do the same in our giving. We should give because of our love for God, our compassion for others and a desire for the gospel to be proclaimed. Jesus also gave with faith in his heart that his sacrificial offering would bring fruit to God. But once again this wasn't selfishly motivated. It was for His Father!

We too should believe in our hearts that our giving, whether financial or otherwise, will result in the furthering of the gospel of the Kingdom, not just what we can benefit from it. If we seek first His Kingdom, then everything we need will be added to us. Our primary pursuit should be the Kingdom of God, not what we want. If this is the case we will have everything we need.

We should give because of our love for God, our compassion for others and a desire for the gospel to be proclaimed

---

So what does Paul mean when he says that *"through Jesus' poverty we might become rich?"* First of all, let me put to rest the argument that Jesus lived a life of financial poverty when he walked the earth. Wise men gave his parents gold, frankincense and myrrh at his birth, enough to easily support their living for years to come, well into Jesus' life and ministry. Understand that there weren't 3 wise men like most manger scenes depict. There were probably hundreds, all of which had their own contributions of these highly valuable commodities. It was the equivalent of winning the lottery!

Apparently, Jesus was doing alright financially because **Matthew 4:13** tells us that after his baptism, he moved out of his mother's house (*"left Nazareth"*) and apparently obtained his own home in Capernaum. (*"Jesus lived in Capernaum"*) The Greek word for live literally means "to reside permanently." A careful look at the gospels reveals that Jesus and his primary disciples came in and out of what the Bible calls *"the house in Capernaum"* for the next 3 ½ years. (**Mt. 9:9-10; Mt. 12:46-13:1; Mk. 2:1-5; Mk.3:19; Mk. 7:1, 14-17; Mk. 9:17, 28-33; Mk. 10:10**)

Scripture also makes it clear that there were several individuals who financially supported his ministry. Jesus was so financially blessed that he was able to provide for his own needs and his disciples too. In fact, he had so much money that he had to have a treasurer (Judas) to keep track of it. I could go on and on, but the point is that the Bible never says that Jesus or his disciples ever lacked a single meal or couldn't pay their bills. Jesus had the resources of heaven at his disposal because he was committed to pleasing his Father and fulfilling his purpose, which was to introduce the Kingdom of heaven to mankind.

Blessed to be a Blessing

Jesus' 'poverty' is rightfully understood by reading **Galatians 3:13**. Jesus became a curse for us so that we would receive the same blessing given to Abraham. Jesus in his divinity (richness) took on humanity (poorness) so that in our humanity we could partake of His divine nature. (**I Peter 1:3-4**) *"He who knew no sin became sin for us"* so we who were sinners by nature could be declared righteous in God's eyes! On that cross, Jesus was stripped of everything including his clothing, His reputation, his earthly ministry and even his own disciples who deserted him. The sins of the world were laid upon him as he took the punishment we all deserve so that we could receive the grace that none of us deserve!

The Hebrew word for bless is *barak,* which means "to speak well of." It also means "to be helped along one's journey." When God blesses, or releases His Word over someone, there are tangible results such as healing, deliverance, restoration and/or prosperity, all of which help people move toward the fulfillment of purpose. (**Psalm 107:20**) By looking at Abraham's life in the Word, you can easily see that God prospered Him financially, but this was just one aspect of God's blessing. The blessing on Abraham's life enabled him to fulfill his divine purpose by giving him access to heavenly resources.

So when Paul tells the Corinthians that "Jesus became poor that we might become rich," he was telling them that they were blessed because Jesus became a curse for us! He used the word rich in the context of financial giving to make the point that there are no limits to God's blessing. Heavenly resources are inexhaustible! The blessing of God's grace enables us to do what we can't do in our own ability. We just need to believe Him to receive it.

> *The blessing of God's grace enables us to do what we can't do in our own ability. We just need to believe Him to receive it*

The Greek word for grace is *charis* which means 'divine influence upon the heart that reflects in one's life.' It also means 'benefit, favor and gift.'   Grace in the New Testament is very similar to what the blessing was in the Old Testament. Both are evidence of the Spirit of God helping people achieve what lies beyond the limitations of their human abilities. And both are accessed by faith. As **Romans 5:2** says, *"We have access by faith into this grace by which we stand."*

Because we have access to God's grace, every area of our lives can and should be positively affected, provided we exercise our faith for forward movement. We are already blessed because we have all received grace from the Lord at new birth as **Ephesians 4:8** describes: *"But to each one of us grace was given."* As we learn to rely upon the ministry of the Holy Spirit within, we will tap into an endless supply of grace and experience *"blessing after blessing."* (**John 1:16**) And as we are faithful to give to others what we have received from the Lord, we will walk in even greater measures of His blessing, *"the abundance of grace"* as **Romans 5:17** puts it!

Grace Makes us Rich!

Allow me to set the record straight: we are rich because we are blessed with His grace! The ministry of the Holy Spirit in our hearts and lives is tangible proof that we are blessed by His grace. **Galatians 3:14** clearly spells this out for us: *"that the blessing given to Abraham might come to the Gentiles through Jesus Christ, so that by faith we might receive the promise of the Spirit."* Because we've received the promise of the Holy Spirit, we can now give to others out of the abundance of grace we've received from the Lord. In essence, grace is the supply of the ministry of the Holy Spirit, both to us and through us to others.

Another Greek word that is closely related to grace (charis) is gift (charisma). It means a 'spiritual endowment or miraculous enablement.' The Holy Spirit in His ministry to us, endows us with supernatural abilities to bless others. This is the grace of God in action through our lives. So when Paul encouraged the Corinthians to *"excel in the grace of giving,"* (**II Cor. 8:7**) his intention was for them to allow the Holy Spirit to move their hearts to give more and more. Not more dollars necessarily, but in a more excellent way: motivated by love for God, compassion for people and a passion for the gospel. They were being encouraged to be sensitive and obedient to the Spirit's concerning their giving, which at times may seem to be beyond their ability in the natural. They were to give because they were already blessed with the grace of the Holy Spirit's guidance, not in order to get blessed.

In essence, grace is the supply of the ministry of the Holy Spirit, both to us and through us to others

---

Financial giving is a very tangible expression of the grace of God in our lives that should mirror the grace Jesus demonstrated by giving his life for us. Love in his heart released grace for all to receive. And grace that we receive can then be released through our giving to activate encouragement and thanksgiving in those we give to, which enables others to do what they couldn't do on their own. And the grace cycle continues... In the words of Jesus, *"freely you have received, so freely give"* and *"it is more blessed to give than to receive."* We are promised an increase of the blessing of grace in our lives as we are faithful to release it to others, whether financially or in the area of our spiritual gifts.

Just so you know, not every member of the church at Corinth became financially independent. But they all received God's grace and thus received God's blessing, which was fully capable of positively impacting their finances, as well as every other area of their lives. You too are blessed with the power of grace if you have received Jesus' wonderful gift of forgiveness and eternal life. May your heart be encouraged to receive the fullness of the ministry of the Holy Spirit, which can change your heart and influence your life in so many dimensions!! Receive His grace and allow it to have its way in your life!

CHAPTER FOUR

Grace is a Person

*"The Word became flesh and made his
dwelling among us. We have seen his glory,
the glory of the One and only, who came
from the Father, full of grace and truth.
From the fullness of his grace we have all
received one blessing after another. For the
law was given through Moses, grace and
truth came through Jesus Christ."*

John 1:14, 16-17

In the last chapter we began by saying what grace is NOT. Now let's explore what grace IS in greater detail. God's grace is more than a spiritual concept to be understood. It's even more than a biblical principle to walk out. First and foremost, grace is a person. His name is Jesus Christ.

Jesus was born in a manger almost 2000 years ago, but Christ existed before the universe was even created. In fact, Christ the Word was the One who created the universe in coordination with the Father's intention and the Spirit's power. The Word later became flesh in the person of Jesus Christ in order to reveal all of God's glory to mankind. The Greek word for glory is *doxa* which basically means 'all that God is and all that God has.' Everything Jesus Christ said and did was intentionally carried out to reveal to us who God is in his multi-faceted splendor.

Not only does God have love to offer us, He is love. (**I John 4:8**) Not only does He have peace to give us, He is our peace. (**Ephesians 2:14**) He not only has truth to share with us, He *is* the truth. (**John 14:6**) And He not only has life to impart to us, He is life itself! (**John 11:25**) Are you getting the picture? Jesus didn't take on human flesh to simply teach us good messages about God's nature. He was the very message himself! He is the very Word that he spoke about. There was no distance between the message he proclaimed and the life he lived.

Everything that God has to offer us is an extension of who He is. Yes, grace is a message to be understood and a power to be received and lived out. But it is first and foremost a person, Jesus Christ. Do you know him? Then you know grace because "*it is by grace you have been saved*." (**Ephesians 2:8**) But do you realize that there is more of him to get to know? Then there also must be more to discover about God's radical grace. The more you learn about His grace, the more you will know Him and become like Him. And the more grace you receive, the more power you will possess to fulfill your purpose.

He is the very Word that He spoke about. There was no distance between the message He proclaimed and the life He lived

Not only is grace a person, but it is also a season. Bible scholars tell us that there are various seasons, better known as ages or dispensations, which define how man can and should relate with God. Each season is initiated and defined by the covenant used to create it. Adam, Noah, Abraham, Moses and Jesus were all key figures who God cut covenant with to initiate new seasons of relationship with God. Each covenant was an improvement on the previous one and contained a greater revelation of who God was, which enabled man to know Him more.

Never take Grace for Granted

It's easy to take for granted the season of grace we are in today. Imagine what it would have been like to live under the previous season of law. We wouldn't have the Spirit of God residing within our spirits. We wouldn't be able to hear God's voice for ourselves. We wouldn't be able to feel His presence. We would also be burdened with over 600 laws that required us to measure up to a standard that was unreachable. And when we didn't measure up (all the time), we would have to sacrifice animals to atone for our sins to alleviate the guilt of disappointing God. On top of that, we would be completely dependent on priests to even have a second-hand relationship with God!

We've got it good! I really don't think we know how good we actually have it. And this is the problem. The majority of the body of Christ today is not acquainted with the pure gospel of grace that was at the forefront of Jesus' ministry. Much of the church is ignorant of the true gospel that the apostle Paul preached on a regular basis. The very meaning of the word 'gospel' is good news but many believers today have received a gospel that is partly good news and partly bad news because they have been introduced to a hybrid of the Old and New Covenants.

The season of grace that governs spiritual activity in the earth today was initiated by Jesus Christ Himself when he died on the cross and rose from the dead. (**Hebrews 9:17**) We understand that the New Covenant is "*a better covenant established on better promises.*" (**Hebrews 8:6**) But the church has had a difficult time understanding the terms of this covenant and has therefore missed out on many of its promises and privileges because of a lack of knowledge. Although all believers have experienced God's saving grace, many get stuck somewhere along the journey to know Him more. Although God has made provision for our total salvation, many believers are ignorant of what Jesus' death on the cross and His resurrection from the dead actually accomplished in its fullness. So they live a partially unfulfilled spiritual life because they don't continue to receive God's grace, "*one blessing after another.*" (**John 1:16**)

Although all believers have experienced God's
saving grace, many get stuck somewhere along
the journey to know Him more

If you feel like you have one foot in the Old Testament and the other one in the New Testament, you're not the only one. The first century church had that difficulty too. With the proclamation of the new gospel of grace came much freedom and much conflict. The message of grace was gladly received by some and yet fought by religious leaders who wanted to hold onto the old way of doing things. This was primarily because their identity and importance had everything to do with people conforming to the law and respecting their position in the old religious system. Embracing 'the new' for leaders in the Old Covenant meant they had to start over like everyone else in the pursuit of the knowledge of God's grace, which most weren't willing to do.

Everything in the law pointed to Jesus and was a prophetic sign of the grace that was to come. For this reason Jesus said that he didn't come to "abolish the law or the Prophets, but to fulfill them." (**Matthew 5:17**) **Colossians 2:17** says it this way: *"these (requirements of the law) are a shadow of the things that were to come, the reality however is found in Christ."* If you notice a shadow, why would you continue to focus on that shadow after the thing it represents comes into plain view? This is exactly what happened with a large number of first century Jews and believers as well. Just as the church of Acts struggled to let go of the works of the law to fully embrace the faith that gave them access to God's grace, we have followed suit.

Mixed-Up Christianity

The other side of the coin is that Jesus *"abolished in his flesh the law with its commandments and regulations."* (**Ephesians 2:15, Colossians 2:14**) On one hand Jesus said that He didn't come to abolish the law and yet this Scripture says the exact opposite! So why the apparent contradiction? The purpose of the law was to bring man to the end of his efforts to earn his own salvation. And because it was impossible for man to measure up to God's standard, God became a man in Jesus Christ to pave the way for man to know God, not based on his own good works, but based on the grace that the finished work of Christ affords us. The law and its regulations no longer need to be carried out in expectation of a coming Messiah because Jesus already came as the fulfillment of every prophetic sign in the law.

The good news is that there is a way out of our mixed-up Christianity and that is by understanding grace as it was originally proclaimed by Jesus Christ Himself and the apostle Paul, who probably had the greatest revelation of grace in his generation. Keep in mind that grace is not just a message, it's a person: Jesus Christ. And grace is more than a spiritual concept. It's the very season we are living in today that has a distinct set of guidelines that inform us how we are to relate with God. Unfortunately, the age of grace we are privileged to live in has been misunderstood for centuries.

The good news is that there is a way out of our mixed-up Christianity and that is by understanding grace as it was originally proclaimed by Jesus Christ Himself

It's amazing to see just how distorted a message can become after it has passed through a number of filters that slightly change its meaning. The telephone game illustrates this perfectly. The person who starts this game says a couple sentences in the ear of the person next to him and then that person repeats what he hears in the ear of the next person. This continues in a circle of people until it reaches the original person who started it. By the time the message passes through a number of different people who relay the message to the next person based on their memory and interpretation of what they hear, it becomes an entirely different message altogether!

This is what tends to happen when truth passes from one generation to the next without the Spirit of grace in control. Man gets his hands on truth and ends up distorting it according to his interpretation, which causes an endless splintering of the body until we reach the place where we are today with over 225 major denominations in the American church alone, not to mention the thousands of independent churches and networks of churches! This is not the result of the Spirit of unity, nor is it the work of God's grace. It is the evidence that the law is alive and well!

Just because the law and all its regulations were nailed to the cross doesn't mean that the power of the law is not still at work today. Living under the law and living under grace are both choices we make by either trusting in our own efforts or by putting our faith in the finished work of Christ. When man trusts in his own ability to interpret the Bible we end up with multiple interpretations that are at odds with each other. But when man trusts in the Spirit to interpret Scripture, we end up with various perspectives that mesh together to form a multifaceted diamond of truth!

Restoring the Foundation of our Nation

The American church is in desperate need of a fresh revelation of the season of grace that we are in today. If we are ever going to bring our nation back to the biblical standards and true Christian values that it was founded upon, we have to first understand the gospel in its purity. The American version of the gospel is a great hindrance to the truth about God's radical grace, which is the very key to our freedom and fulfillment in God. We need to hear the truth from the originator of truth Himself, not just from the person next to us in the telephone game circle.

Paul encountered this exact conflict in the culture of his day. When he realized that the gospel was being polluted in the minds of the Galatians, he addressed them rather bluntly. He comments in **Galatians 1:6**, "*I am astonished that you are so quickly deserting the One who called you by the grace of Christ and are turning to a different gospel, which is really no*

50

gospel at all. Evidently some people are throwing you into confusion and are trying to pervert the gospel of Christ."

When law is mixed with grace, the message of the gospel (good news) becomes tarnished. This is what happened with the Galatian believers. They began to embrace once again the requirements of the law that were fulfilled by Christ and done away with. What they didn't realize was that this was a slap in the face of God. Attempting to earn their own righteousness by the works of the law made Christ's sacrifice on the cross useless and powerless in their lives! If their own religious efforts could make them righteous, then why did Jesus have to suffer on the cross?

"I do not set aside the grace of God, for if righteousness could be gained through the law, Christ died for nothing." Galatians 2:21

"It is for freedom that Christ has set us free. Stand firm, then, and do not let yourselves be burdened again by a yoke of slavery. Mark my words! I, Paul, tell you that if you let yourselves be circumcised, Christ will be of no value to you at all. Again I declare to every man who lets himself be circumcised that he is obligated to obey the whole law. You who are trying to be justified by law have been alienated from Christ; you have fallen from grace." Galatians 5:1-4

You might be thinking right about now: "this really doesn't apply to me because I'm not considering getting circumcised or sacrificing any animals in my backyard anytime soon!" However, you may be attempting to live by man-made rules that conform to religious cultures that are not endorsed by the Spirit. Or possibly by trying to meet self-imposed expectations that hinder the Holy Spirit's ministry in your life. Or perhaps you're pursuing good things for the wrong reasons, to impress others or to feel good about yourself. Law can take on many shapes and sizes. Truthfully, it boils down to whether you are relying on the grace of God and the leading of the Holy Spirit or not. Spiritually speaking, if you can do what you do without the assistance of the Holy Spirit, then you are functioning based on law, which makes Christ of no value to you.

Think about it: Jesus nailed to his cross all 613 laws from the Old Covenant and made it possible for the Spirit of God to dwell in every born again believer. He wants all of us to hear His voice for ourselves and to be led by His Spirit. That way, He can write His laws on our hearts and make us living epistles. If we look to external rules to measure up to, we are at the same time neglecting the ministry of the Spirit of grace within. And by doing so, we are trying to earn our own righteousness by our good works instead of trusting that Jesus' blood was enough. And when we insist on doing things without His grace, we are in essence telling God that we don't need His help, we got this!

Spiritually speaking, if you can do what you do without the assistance of the Holy Spirit, then you are functioning based on law, which makes Christ of no value to you

You may have never viewed religious activity in this way before, but it is what it is, the greatest opposition to the grace God has deposited in your spirit. Going through the motions brings the work of the Spirit to a standstill in your life. In fact, the more religious you become, the less grace is able to operate in your heart and the less the Holy Spirit is free be Himself in your life. Our religious ways ultimately hinder Him from fulfilling His ministry to, in and through us!

One aspect of the ministry of the Holy Spirit is to lead you into all truth. This includes leading you away from religious thinking that is hindering your spiritual progress. So tune your spiritual ears to the voice of the Spirit. He will help navigate you through the traditions and doctrines of men you may have inherited, which will prepare you to acquire a fresh revelation of who He is and what He has to offer you. And as you follow His lead, fresh grace will be released into your life, activating you towards your purpose in ways you never dreamed possible!

CHAPTER FIVE

Spiritual Responsibility

"Finally, be strong in the Lord and in his mighty power. Put on the full armor of God so that you can take your stand against the devil's schemes." **Ephesians 6:10-11**

Most Christians interpret spiritual responsibility in the framework of leadership roles. Although ministering to others is important, it is secondary to ministering to yourself. What I'm referring to is the need to take care of your own spirit. How can you edify others if you aren't built up yourself? How can you encourage someone else if you are discouraged? We need to follow in the steps of King David who *"encouraged himself in the Lord."* Jesus said to *"love your neighbor as you love yourself."* Simply put, you can't give something that you don't have.

As human beings, we have various responsibilities in life. I define responsibility as "the ability to respond to a need by making sure it gets met." Having a need and taking responsibility to meet that need are two very different things. We all need physical exercise, but how many of us really respond accordingly to that need to see that it is met? We all need to eat healthy foods, but the tendency is to eat what tastes good instead of what is actually good for us. We all bear financial responsibility for our lives, but many of us are in debt up to our eyeballs because we spend more money than we make and don't exercise the discipline to deny ourselves instant gratification for future financial security.

Take a moment to think of all the physical, financial and relational responsibilities that you have, as well as your responses to those needs. We all have a lot on our plates! But the most important and often-neglected responsibility pertains to the condition of your spirit. One thing is for sure, responsibilities don't just take care of themselves. You have to take the initiative to get things done! When you're hungry, the refrigerator door doesn't open of its own accord and send a hamburger floating through the air to find you! Tires don't just change themselves when the tread gets thin! And dirty diapers don't just vanish! You have to do something about the needs in your life.

If you haven't been taking spiritual responsibility for your spirit recently, your spiritual condition is not up to par, which can open the door for distraction, deception or possibly even destruction

---

It's time for you to respond aggressively to your spirit's need for spiritual sustenance on a daily basis. Just because you've been born again doesn't mean that your spirit is in good shape today. And just because you go to church doesn't necessarily mean that your spiritual condition is top notch either. If you haven't been taking spiritual responsibility for your spirit recently, your spiritual condition is not up to par, which can open the door for distraction, deception or possibly even destruction.

You Can't Win if You Don't Play by the Rules

If you don't take the initiative to obey **Ephesians 6:10**- *"be strong in the Lord,"* you will lack the ability to overcome the devil's schemes as portrayed in **Ephesians 6:11**. What your spirit needs more than anything is a consistent flow of spiritual life and strength that only comes from the Holy Spirit. The Holy Spirit began this work in you the moment you were born again and desires to continue depositing heaven's life into your spirit throughout your life. But you have to take the initiative to see that happen!

Something that is important for you to understand is that your spirit is very dynamic as opposed to being static. What I mean is that it has ebbs and flows like the ocean. The environments you engage with, that which you expose your spirit to, has a tremendous effect on your spirit's overall condition. What becomes a stronghold in your soul due to consistent exposure to negative influence, can hinder the free flow of your spirit as well as contaminate your spiritual well. But a renewed mind and a heart after God can open the door for your spirit to be cleansed and to soar to higher heights than you've ever experienced in Him!

The environments you engage with, that which you expose your spirit to, has a tremendous effect on your spirit's overall condition

The strength level of your spirit can be high or low depending on a number of factors, all of which depend on you taking responsibility to care for your spirit. That's why God commands us to *"be strong in the Lord."* It's our responsibility! God isn't going to do it all for us. We have a part to play. Don't get me wrong, you can't have a spirit in good condition apart from God's assistance, but your cooperation with the Spirit of God is a key component that can't be neglected!

Your spirit is very much like a muscle. It needs food, exercise and rest. The Scripture says that *"faith comes by hearing God's Word."* A key ingredient to giving nutrients to your spirit lies in hearing God's voice and meditating on what He has said to you. Notice that I said hearing God's voice, NOT reading the Bible. There is a huge difference!

The Word is Faith Food

The Bible is a God-inspired collection of books that contains stories of real people who were genuinely touched and changed by God's voice. If you allow the One who inspired the writing of the Bible to interpret it and apply it to your life, then God's Word (in the Bible) will feed your spirit. But if you simply read the Bible with your mind without the Spirit's guidance, it will only supply you with historical facts and information instead of spiritual life and revelation.

In addition to the personal study of God's Word and listening for His still small voice, it is important to engage in meaningful fellowship on a regular basis. As the **Proverb** says, *"iron sharpens iron."* Spiritual encouragement is contagious, so get around people whose spirits are sensitive to the Spirit and full of the Word. Also, submit yourself to people who can minister to you in leadership roles. Impartation is a powerful principle where strength in one persons' spirit is transferred to another by way of Biblical preaching, discipleship, prayer and the laying on of hands.

Your spirit also needs exercise. What you feed it needs an outlet for application. Just as natural food gives your body strength so it can work, God's strength in your spirit enables you to accomplish spiritual things. The first spiritual work you should be committed to is prayer, which is fueled and directed by God's voice. We are commanded to *"pray in the Spirit at all times."* This may mean different things for different people, but one thing is for sure, our prayers are to be led by the Spirit in agreement with His Word. If we pray according to His will, we exercise our faith for God to move on our behalf. When our words agree with God's Word to us and our spirit is fueled by the power of the Spirit, prayer strengthens our spirit and changes situations.

Give Your Spirit a Good Meal and a Nap

The second spiritual work of your spirit has to do with obeying what God has spoken to you. Carrying out God's orders to completion with the right attitude and motivation will undoubtedly create room in your spirit for the next revelation. But a sure way to block God's revelation in your spirit is to NOT be a doer of His Word. Why should God continue to unveil truth to you if you don't do anything with it?

The third spiritual work of your spirit has to do with ministering to others. As your spirit is engaged in helping others with what God has helped you with, you will notice that your spirit will increase in spiritual life. I can't tell you how many times I've felt my spirit recharged after mentoring someone or ministering the Word of God to people. As you pour into the lives of others what God has deposited within you, there is a downpour from heaven back into your spirit.

And just as much as your spirit needs food and exercise, it also needs rest. This is not inactivity, but an active communion with the Lord in praise and worship. Just being in His presence brings refreshing to your spirit that comes no other way. Spiritual fatigue is replaced by spiritual vitality when you truly worship God in spirit and truth. Engaging your emotions and intellect in worship goes a long way in allowing the Holy Spirit to do a deep work in your spirit.

Spiritual fatigue is replaced by spiritual vitality when you truly worship God in spirit and truth

The responsibility is yours. Feed your spirit. Exercise your spirit. Rest your spirit. And the Holy Spirit will continue to develop your spiritual life so you can be one with Him, one with His church and useful in reaching others for Christ. Don't wait until your tank is on empty to refuel! As soon as you notice your gauge moving downward, move upward towards heaven! If you do your part, He will do His part!

"Come near to God and He will come near to you!" **James 4:8**

CHAPTER SIX

Because I Said So

*"For the word of God is living and active.
Sharper than any double-edged sword, it
penetrates to dividing soul and spirit, joints
and marrow; it judges the thoughts and
attitudes of the heart."* **Hebrews 4:12**

'Because I said so!' Every child on the planet has probably heard this at one time or another growing up. And every parent has probably said this in response to the proverbial question 'why?' This question is sometimes asked from a sincere heart that is seeking to make sense out of certain situations in life. But at other times it is projected on authority figures as a challenge to convince them as to why they should do what they are told to do.

When the question 'why?' is followed up by the infamous answer 'because I said so,' this can mean a number of things. It could simply mean that the parent doesn't exactly know the answer. Or maybe it's a lazy excuse for not wanting to take the time to teach or explain something. Or perhaps it could mean that they want to be obeyed without being questioned altogether. And then there are those moments when there simply isn't enough time for an explanation just right then. But sadly enough, the necessary explanation is all-too-often swept under the rug of the next 'because I said so.' And the cycle continues...

Unfortunately, this expression has taught myriads of children that authority figures aren't always transparent with their subordinates and in some instances, that blind obedience is expected from those under their influence. My belief is that this mindset has crept into the church. Many times we are told to do certain things without sound biblical understanding as to why we should do them. We are commonly told *what* to do and are often given a particular version of *how* to do things, but the *why* is often neglected when a clear explanation is in order.

Of course, the 'why' of spiritual obedience should always be substantiated by the Word of God. Church doctrines (*what to believe*) and religious traditions (*how to do things*) carved in the stones of church services and organizational structures are not reason enough to obey. We need chapter and verse (*why*). Anything other than the Word of God which serves as a foundation for what we believe and how we live is a shaky foundation, which is sure to fall under the pressures of life.

We are commonly told what to do and are often given a particular version of how to do things, but the why is often neglected when a clear explanation is in order

---

Even Jesus didn't pull the 'because I said so' card. He derived his authority from the word of God coming to him from the Father (**Matthew 4:4**). In fact, he only spoke what he heard the Father speaking to him. And he only did what he saw the Father doing. So when Jesus issued orders to his disciples, he actually did this because he discerned what the Father was saying and doing in their lives, and he wanted them to experience the Father's love. Jesus then took the time to help them understand some things along the way, but they had a difficult time fully grasping some truths until they received the Holy Spirit on the Day of Pentecost.

No New Testament? No Problem!

So the saga continues. For example, we are told that in order to be good Christians we should read our Bibles every day. But why? "Because I said so." OK, that's not going to cut it anymore. "Well, because the Bible itself says to." That's better but really, *why* should we read the word of God? What specifically should motivate us to study the Scriptures? And what tangible results should we expect as a result of becoming a diligent student of the Word?

Before we look in the Word to answer these questions, ponder this for a moment: believers in the first century DID NOT read their Bibles every day, and yet they experienced exponential spiritual and numerical growth as the gospel of the kingdom was proclaimed in their generation. You might be scratching your head at this statement, wondering how this could be true! Allow me to explain.

For starters, the New Testament was still in the process of being written in the first century and wasn't compiled for quite some time after that. Secondly, the printing press wasn't invented as of yet, so copies of the Old Testament weren't exactly accessible in the local Christian bookstores. And thirdly, the vast majority of people in the Roman Empire at that time were illiterate, and therefore couldn't read the Bible even if they had one! For these very reasons, the reading of Scripture took precedence in their public meetings.

Believers in the first century DID NOT read their Bibles every day, and yet they experienced exponential spiritual and numerical growth as the gospel of the kingdom was proclaimed in their generation

---

I am NOT making the case that we don't need to read the Word. My point is that the early church thrived under the leading of the Spirit despite the lack of the Word's availability to them. With our ability to read and our easy access to the Old and New Testaments, how much more of an impact should we be making in the world in which we live?

We have the same Spirit that the early church had, the very Spirit that raised Jesus from the dead, and yet our ability to transform our world pales in comparison to the first century believers. How can this be so? Now that's a good question that deserves a good answer! I'll take a stab at that one a little later. But for now, let's dive into some biblical reasons why every believer should diligently read and study God's Word.

So Why Read the Word?

We are *all* priests and kings (**I Peter 2:5,9** & **Revelation 1:5,6**) and therefore have a responsibility to (1) maintain our own spiritual health (**Matthew 4:4, I Timothy 4:11-16**) and to (2) position ourselves to hear from God on behalf of others (**Colossians 3:16, I Corinthians 14:31**). The Word of God assists us with both of these endeavors.

God never intended for a special class of people to do all the studying and interpreting of the Word while the rest of us are spoon-fed whatever comes our way! One of the aspects of the New Covenant that Jeremiah prophesied about is that we would ALL know Him, "from the least to the greatest." The Word of God reveals God's nature and His will, which enables us to (3) progress in our knowledge of Him, which ultimately enables us to live a productive life. So if you want to know Him more and for God to make Himself known through your life, then a steady diet of the Word is vital.

God never intended for a special class of people to do all the studying and interpreting of the Word while the rest of us are spoon-fed whatever comes our way!

Pursuing a greater knowledge of God's Word is also pivotal to the (4) "renewing of our minds," (**Romans 12:1, Ephesians 4:23**) which is presented as a continual process that requires continual pursuit. God's thoughts have a way of transforming our thoughts when we allow the Spirit to illuminate His truth to us, even truth that He spoke to past generations. This is possible because "the word of God is living and powerful." (**Hebrews 4:12**)

Closely related to the renewal of the mind is the need to (5) counteract the influence of the world with the power of God's Word. The culture in which we live bombards us daily with beliefs, practices, priorities and values that are contrary to God's will for our lives. In order to recognize these things before they conform us to worldly standards, we must become familiar with the culture of heaven, which is revealed through the Word of God. We need to be mindful of our kingdom citizenship and to be reminded of the values of the kingdom that should determine how we live our lives.

Another important reason that believers today should be consistent readers of the Word of God is to (6) familiarize themselves with Scripture so as to detect false teaching when they hear it. The fact that the New Testament warns believers numerous times of false leaders who will bring false teachings into the church in the last days should motivate us to take measures to safeguard against this deception. (**Matthew 24:4-5, I Timothy 4:1, II Peter 2:1-3**)   Deception is more likely to take place in people who are unfamiliar with the truth of God's Word than in those who are familiar with the Scriptures. That's why Jesus said "watch out that no one deceive you." (**Matthew 24:4**)   Paul said it this way in **Colossians 2:8**- "See to it that no one takes you captive through hollow and deceptive philosophy..." The only way to detect counterfeit money is to be familiar with the real thing!

From Inspiration to Interpretation

Notice that I didn't list 'the accumulation of biblical knowledge' as a reason to read the Word. The Bible is a spiritual book and therefore should be treated differently than every other book on the shelf. Reading the Bible without the inspiration of the Holy Spirit can actually be counterproductive! Paul said in **I Corinthians 8:1** that *"knowledge puffs up."* When spiritual life takes a back seat to biblical knowledge, you're on the road to spiritual stagnation and pride. Knowledge is a tool in the hands of the Holy Spirit, but without the Holy Spirit it can be a weapon of mass destruction.

> *Reading the Bible without the inspiration of the Holy Spirit can actually be counterproductive!*

Many Christians make the mistake of judging their own spirituality based on their biblical knowledge or past spiritual experience. And that is exactly the moment that pride develops in believers, becoming a hindrance to receiving and walking in the newness of life that is available through the Word. The Word is a powerful tool but please understand that if it was written through the inspiration of the Spirit, then it must be read with revelation from the Spirit. The Holy Spirit is our Teacher. Don't read the Bible without Him.

In review, here's why we should read the Word. Allow these reasons to motivate you to sit in the classroom of the Spirit, explore the holy textbook with fresh hunger and walk out the wisdom revealed to you in your everyday life!

1. Maintain your spiritual health
2. Position yourself to hear from God for others
3. Progress in your knowledge of God

4. Renew your mind
5. Counteract the world's influence
6. Protect yourself from false teaching

CHAPTER SEVEN

Half the Bible, Twice the Impact!?

"From everyone who has been given much,
much will be demanded." **Luke 12:48**

"Now it is required that those who have been
given a trust must prove faithful."

I Corinthians 4:2

God is a giver. He's a giver because He's a lover. He loved us so much, He gave us His Son. After His Son gave his life for us he rose from the dead, ascended back to heaven and gave the Spirit the responsibility to help us receive all that God has given us. He gave us His Word to reveal His intention to freely give us all good things. He gave us His Spirit, not only to make us aware of heaven's possibilities, but to help us walk in their reality here on earth.

We love Him because He first loved us. Everything we have of value came from Him and therefore everything we have to give is in response to what He has given us. We aren't initiators, we are responders. We respond to what God initiates in our lives. God gave us faith, not so we could use it at our discretion to get what we want, but so we could believe His Word and walk into the reality of His intention. Faith gives us access into His grace, which encompasses all that He is and all that He has for us.

God gave us faith, not so we could use it at our discretion to get what we want, but so we could believe His Word and walk into the reality of His intention

---

Faith is quite possibly the most pivotal gift we have been given by God. Faith gives us the ability to hear His voice, believe His Word and receive newness of life that only comes from heaven. Exercising our faith in God through vocal proclamation and by active obedience enables us to participate in God's supernatural life in the midst of our everyday lives.

Faith causes us to recognize the spiritual world around us and to participate in its reality by embracing and releasing the creative power of His Word. The universe was framed by the Word of God and our world can likewise be formed and reformed by the words of our mouth as we agree with heaven and welcome the kingdom of God into our lives.

A Lifestyle of Repentance

The beauty of the Word of God is that it <u>inspires our souls</u> to live above the challenges of life and at the same time <u>energizes our spirits</u> to break through barriers that limit God's influence in and through us. This is possible because the Word both imparts faith (**Romans 10:17**) and activates the faith we already have. (**Romans 10:8-10**)

With half the Bible we currently possess, the early church made twice the impact on their world than we have thus far. Allow me to submit to you that this is true because they were faithful to respond aggressively to what they were entrusted with: the great commission to preach the gospel of the kingdom and to disciple nations with kingdom principles that make our lives noticeably better here on earth. In order for our generation to experience God's kingdom the way He intends, we need a radical paradigm shift in our westernized thinking. We need to be delivered from a culture that places us at the center of attention. Church life is not about what we can get out of it, it is supposed to be all about Him!

Last time I checked, Jesus promised to build His church on the foundation of His Word through the ministry of the Spirit, who is the executive director of the kingdom of God in the earth. The Spirit develops heavenly culture in our lives as we allow Him to carve away earthly culture that stands in opposition to His ways. This is what it means to "*repent, for the kingdom of heaven is at hand,*" (**Matthew 3:2, Matthew 4:17, Matthew 10:7, Acts 2:37-40**) which by the way, was the predominant message of John the Baptist (the last OT prophet), Jesus (the initiator of the New Covenant) and the early church.

Repentance, which is a continual change of mind and lifestyle, is an absolute requirement to experience greater depths of God's kingdom in our lives. The atmosphere of heaven permeates the hearts of those who submit to repentance as the Spirit leads them into all truth. Repentance is not just something we do in order to be born again or something we do in response to an awareness of our sins. Repentance is the life-long process of submitting our thoughts to God's thoughts. And the Word of God is a tremendous tool God has given us to help with this endeavor.

The atmosphere of heaven permeates the hearts of those who submit to repentance as the Spirit leads them into all truth

---

One clear distinction between the church we read about in the book of Acts and today's church is the approach to God's Word. To believe something in A.D. 50 implied immediate obedience and life application. After all, *"faith without works is dead."* But we tend to separate our beliefs from our actions today. This is primarily due to our tendency to *"lean on our own understanding instead of trusting in the Lord"* to help us walk things out. (**Proverbs 3:5-6**) In today's religious culture, it seems like we place greater importance on what feels spiritual to us and appears spiritual to others, rather than what is truly spiritual in the eyes of God.

Plastic Christians

This generation is full of professional church-going, sermon-listening, conference-attending, book-reading Christians who equate the accumulation of their biblical knowledge to spiritual maturity. But spiritual maturity is not measured by the Word of God we are familiar with. It is evident by the God of the Word that we intimately know and are influenced by.

Another noticeable difference between the church of today and that of yesterday lies in the dependence on the ministry of the Holy Spirit. Due to persecution and civil unrest, first century believers depended on the wisdom and protection of the Lord for their very survival. And due to the fact that they had limited access to the Scriptures, they were forced to rely on the Spirit within to verify truth when they heard it. Due to our abundant access to Scripture, I think we depend too much on our ability to process information instead of the Spirit's ministry to reveal truth to us.

Spiritual maturity is not measured by the Word of God we are familiar with. It is evident by the God of the Word that we intimately know and are influenced by

In our lush Christian culture we tend to conveniently fit our church life into our weekly routine, but in the early church it was a way of life. Their focus wasn't on fulfilling expected Christian duties, checking them off their religious boxes. It was set on engaging their relationship with God and others on a daily basis because they were compelled to do so by the love of Christ. Because they relied so heavily on the Spirit's ministry from day to day, the Spirit was able to form Christ in them and reveal Christ through them in rapid acceleration, so much that they turned their world upside-down in a relatively short time span!

If we can learn and apply just these two lessons from the early church, we too will turn our world upside-down. We shouldn't read our Bibles with the religious spectacles of our idolatrous culture because we will end up deifying the apostles of old. They were ordinary men and women just like you and I who seriously embraced their responsibility to be faithful to the Word and to the Spirit who inspired it in the first place.

Each generation has the luxury of learning from previous generations who have experienced God firsthand. In its simplest form, the Word of God is a collection of stories detailing how generations of old came into relationship with God because they responded to the voice of God in the midst of their frail humanity. Welcome the fullness of the Spirit's ministry within as you continue your quest to know Him more through His magnificent Word!

CHAPTER EIGHT

Can You Hear Me Now?   -God

"And when he brings out his own sheep, he
goes before them; and the sheep follow him,
for they know his voice."   **John 10:4**

Jesus once told a parable about a flock of sheep and their shepherd, illustrating the normalcy of Christians to hear the voice of God for themselves. In this parable He made it clear that healthy believers not only listen for the voice of God, but they understand it and respond to it accordingly. Hearing God's voice in every season of life should be the norm for believers today, but if you were to ask a handful of Christians what God is speaking to them about, the majority of them would most likely shrug their shoulders and say like a little child, "I don't know." This is especially sad for those who have been in relationship with God for 20+ years.

You would think that after getting to know God for a number of years and hearing His voice time and time again that believers would become more sensitive to His voice and be able to recognize what God is trying to convey to them at any given moment. But unfortunately that is often not the case! It's one thing to be married and another thing altogether to be happily married, which involves consistent communication and cooperation to achieve. So just because someone has been a born again believer for a long time doesn't guarantee that they are a mature Christian who has fully developed their ability to hear God's voice.

Healthy believers not only listen for the voice of God, but they understand it and respond to it accordingly

---

Hearing the voice of God is elementary to the Christian life and is foundational for spiritual maturity. The Scripture also says that *"those who are led by the Spirit are the sons of God."* This verse actually means that believers can be classified as mature sons of God when they learn to follow the leading of the Spirit in their lives, which starts with hearing His voice. How can someone follow the Spirit's leading if they can't tell where He is taking them? Hearing God's voice is imperative if we want to download orders from headquarters and fulfill His purpose for our lives.

You are blessed with spiritual leadership, the Word of God and the Holy Spirit Himself to help train you to hear the voice of God. If you consistently receive the Word of God from spiritual leadership that God has assigned for your life, you will notice a pattern of accuracy, timeliness and freshness in your spirit. It's absolutely amazing how the Holy Spirit can speak through people in a pastoral and prophetic manner that obviously is above human effort. If this is not the case, perhaps you are misplaced in the body of Christ or you are not conditioning yourself to hear God's voice through your leadership. Your ability to hear God's voice should definitely increase as you receive words from the Lord from your leadership that are specific enough to accurately deal with the issues of your life.

The Value of His Voice

The Word of God is actually a compilation of stories about countless people who heard the voice of God for themselves and whose lives were forever changed. God can and will use these stories from the Bible to encourage and teach you, which will form the basis for what He will speak specifically to you and what He wants to do in your life. If you allow Him to, He will breathe on particular passages of Scripture that directly apply to situations in your life. The principles of truth in God's Word will safeguard you against deception and will help you discern the voice of God, which will be in line with the truth already revealed in His Word.

Perhaps the most important factor in hearing God's voice is the Holy Spirit Himself, Who lives inside of every born again believer. The Bible says that He only speaks to us what He hears from the Father. He reminds us of <u>what He has already spoken</u> to us, teaches us <u>present truth</u> and shows us <u>things to come</u>. The Spirit of truth has been commissioned to lead and guide us into all truth, which is a progressive journey from where we have been to where He wants to take us. When you stop and think about it, the success of the early church wasn't due to receiving encouragement from the New Testament because they didn't have one to depend on. But they did have the Holy Spirit, and Scripture makes it clear that they made it their ambition to hear His voice and follow His lead on a consistent basis.

---

*What we need more than anything is to place
our dependence on the Spirit of God to lead and
guide us in our daily lives*

I think our religious culture makes it easy to depend on others to gather the 'manna' that we should be gathering for ourselves on a daily basis. After all, that's what we pay pastors to do, right? Wrong!! In one sense, our Bibles make it easier to lean on our understanding rather than the person of the Holy Spirit. Even an unbeliever can gather information from the Bible without the assistance of the Holy Spirit.

Don't get me wrong, we need spiritual leadership and the protection that the Word of God affords us. But what we need more than anything is to place our dependence on the Spirit of God to lead and guide us in our daily lives. He should be the One inspiring our leadership to speak to us. And besides that, He authored the Word of God in the first place! If He inspired men to write the Scriptures, then He can inspire us to understand them, provided we submit to His rightful place in our lives.

Selective Hearing

One of the biggest hindrances I see that keeps people from hearing the voice of God is what is known as 'selective hearing.' Have you ever met someone who selects what they want to hear and remember while conveniently forgetting about everything else? Some Christians treat the Scriptures this way and also treat the Spirit of God in the same manner, welcoming words of comfort and encouragement while rejecting words of correction and instruction.

Paul told the Thessalonians to *"quench not the Spirit,"* which means to not hinder the activity of the Spirit in any way. Who are we to tell Him what He can say to us? And why would we refuse to hear what He wants us to know? Perhaps we're holding onto some things that we need to let go of, or possibly neglecting to embrace what He has already revealed to us. If we continue to resist the voice of the Spirit in our lives, we will gradually lose our ability to hear His voice altogether. That's why **Hebrews 3:15** says *"today, if you will hear His voice, do not harden your hearts."* It's a dangerous thing to turn a deaf ear to the Lord!

The most repeated verse in the New Testament is this: *"he that has an ear to hear, let him hear what the Spirit says to the churches."* This verse implies that the Spirit is talking and it is our responsibility to hear what He is saying. We are presumptuous if we believe that if God wants to tell us something, then bless God, He will just get our attention! It is our responsibility to create the right kind of environment, to position ourselves so we can hear what He is saying, understand what He means and respond to His Word accordingly. If we do this on a consistent basis, we will grow spiritually and begin to hear God's voice for others.

It is our responsibility to create the right kind of environment, to position ourselves so we can hear what He is saying, understand what He means and respond to His Word accordingly

---

Welcome the voice of God in your life, trusting that God knows what you need to hear, when you need to hear it. Listen for His voice all around you, especially through the Word of God and your spiritual leadership. But more than anything, ask the Lord to sensitize your heart to the voice of the Spirit within, the Spirit of truth. With greater sensitivity to His voice, you will recognize Him speaking to you through people and in ways you wouldn't ordinarily expect! Take the limits off heaven's desire to communicate what you need to know and you will be equipped to fulfill your spiritual assignment. Respond to His voice and you will never be the same! All because of His still small voice.

CHAPTER NINE

The Wilderness, the Mountain, the Garden and the Cross

"After Jesus said this, he looked toward heaven and prayed: Father, the time has come. Glorify your Son that your Son may glorify you." **John 17:1**

As the Son of God, Jesus came to reveal who God the Father is. But as the Son of Man, Jesus demonstrated how we can walk in relationship with the Father. It's all-too-easy to assume that the supernatural life and ministry of Jesus were a result of his divinity, but keep in mind that he didn't do any miracles until the Spirit came upon him after his baptism at the age of 30. Jesus even said that he couldn't do or say anything that he didn't first sense his Father leading and empowering him to accomplish. The divinity of God was revealed through the humanity of Christ, and the same opportunity awaits us today.

It's amazing when you think about it. We're also called sons of God and are given the same invitation to participate in God's life that Jesus demonstrated for us. It only makes sense: if Jesus depended on the Father for a continual supply of divine life, then so should we. Unlike the children of Israel in the wilderness, divine life didn't fall from the sky for Jesus to find and eat. Jesus had to make a concerted effort to get away from the multitudes, and even away from his closest disciples at times, to maintain his connection with the Father through consistent prayer.

Scripture gives us insight into the prayer life of Jesus which should inspire us to follow in his footsteps. If Jesus did miracles because of his divinity then there wouldn't have been a need to stay connected to the Father through prayer. But that is not the case. Consider this: **Luke 5:16** reveals that Jesus "*often withdrew into the wilderness and prayed*." Prayer wasn't something that he occasionally did as the need arose. It was something he consistently did because he knew that as a man he needed God's strength, refreshing and guidance to fully participate in divine life, which enabled him to resist temptation and to fulfill God's will.

It only makes sense: if Jesus depended on the Father for a continual supply of divine life, then so should we

---

We know that Jesus spent 40 days praying in the wilderness in preparation for his ministry, which actually set a precedent for the next few years. It was this same wilderness that Jesus returned to time and time again, knowing that "*man doesn't live by bread alone, but by every word that proceeds from the mouth of God.*" Jesus made it a priority to talk to God and to listen for His voice because he knew that there is life-giving power in God's words.

Whether God's words are heard, meditated on, confessed, prayed, prophesied, sung, taught or proclaimed, they have inherent power to give life to situations. Living off yesterday's Word will eventually lose its power just as the manna gathered by the Israelites grew stale if it wasn't consumed within 24 hours. That's why it's important to hear what God is saying today. *"Today, if you will hear his voice..."* (**Hebrews 3:7**)

When Jesus sensed a need in his human spirit for a divine reload, he attempted to find a quiet place but the crowds often hunted him down and made it difficult to get alone with the Father. But he persevered nonetheless and found both time and a place to spend with God. There is an obvious lesson to be learned and applied here. There are many hindrances to prayer, the majority of which are not evil in and of themselves. Even noble tasks need to be set aside at times for the priority of receiving divine life from the Lord. The only way to serve the Lord *"in newness of spirit"* and walk *"in newness of life"* is by receiving fresh manna from the Living Bread.

Mountaintop Experiences

Then there were special times Jesus spent on the mountain with the Lord, sometimes all night long. **Luke 6:12** says this was the case the night prior to Jesus choosing and identifying the twelve disciples from the larger group of disciples. On another occasion Jesus took Peter, James and John with him to the mountain for a season of overnight prayer on what is known as the 'mount of transfiguration.' Toward the end of his earthly ministry Jesus taught in the temple by day, but at night He stayed on the Mount of Olives (**Luke 21:37**). **Luke 22:39** says that this became his regular custom, most likely in preparation for what he knew was his last season of ministry. He probably needed some focused prayer time prior to fulfilling His ultimate mission on the cross.

Jesus' regular place of prayer transitioned from the wilderness to the mountain. The wilderness was the place he attended to his need for spiritual life whereas the mountain was the place he prepared himself to release that life to others. The more spiritual life Jesus received from the Father, the more that life spilled over into the lives of others through his ministry. Make it your ambition to establish your 'wilderness prayer life' for your own good and your 'mountain prayer life' for the good of those you minister to.

It's interesting to note the special privilege Jesus extended to his closest disciples by bringing them with him to the mount of transfiguration. Also, he let them know where he was praying at other times so they could find him if need be. He kept this information private because of the crowds. For example, after feeding the 5000 "*Jesus was praying alone and his disciples joined him*" because they knew right where he was at (**Luke 9:17-18**). Also, **Luke 11:1** tells us that "*as He was praying in a certain place, when He ceased, one of His disciples said to Him, Lord, teach us to pray...*" Once again, they knew right where he was. This speaks of the importance of having a select number of people in your life that you can trust to pray with and for you during critical times.

The more spiritual life Jesus received from the Father, the more that life spilled over into the lives of others through his ministry

---

Jesus placed great importance on getting away from the endless needs of people in order to get his own needs met by the Father. This made it possible for his spiritual strength to be replenished, enabling him to minister to other people once again. It also seems that he thought it was important enough to involve his disciples in his prayer life so they could get a glimpse of what dynamic interaction with the Father looks like. It was through this access into his prayer life that his disciples developed a hunger to know God for themselves. Hence, they asked him to teach them to pray. And Jesus did just that.

He gave them an understanding that prayer isn't just our way of getting God to do what we want Him to do, twisting His arm to meet our needs. Prayer is the opportunity to become acquainted with Him and to be transformed into His image, thus empowering us to make Him known to others. It is the connection between heaven and earth that serves as a bridge for God to manifest His glory in the earth.

Excruciating Pain in an Extravagant Garden

Then there was the garden, the garden of Gethsemane. You actually had to climb the Mount of Olives first to get to this special place near Jerusalem, where Jesus often met with his disciples. This happened to be one of those places that Jesus allowed a few disciples to join him and where the others could reach him if need be. It was there that Peter, James and John were enlightened to the fact that without divine life surging on the inside, they couldn't even stay awake to support Jesus in prayer. It was there that Jesus surrendered his will to the Father in regard to laying down his life for us. It was there that Peter resisted the arrest of Jesus by cutting off the ear of the high priests' servant. It was there that the beginning of the end took place.

Jesus knew that he didn't have it in him to follow through with Calvary without a fresh dose of God's life and strength. When Jesus surrendered his will to the Father, a divine exchange took place, giving him the passion to persevere all the way to the empty tomb. Having finished praying, his betrayer located him and handed him over to the chief priests. He didn't resist because he knew it was part of God's plan. He learned that prayer was just as much about submitting to the Father's will as it was in speaking forth His will to change circumstances.

While Jesus received divine life in the wilderness and received spiritual power to minister to others in the mountain, he surrendered his will to the Father in the garden and thus received power to overcome resistance to fulfilling his purpose. The garden elevated the trust Jesus had in the Father's plan despite what he understood or desired. We too need to surrender our plans and desires to the Lord in our 'garden of prayer,' trusting that He knows what is best for us and for His Kingdom. Submitting to His thoughts and ways is never easy, but it yields incredible results because by doing so we receive the grace to persevere through trying circumstances, all the way to our 'empty tomb!'

Jesus knew that he didn't have it in him to follow through with Calvary without a fresh dose of God's life and strength. When Jesus surrendered his will to the Father, a divine exchange took place, giving him the passion to persevere all the way to the empty tomb

As Jesus hung on the cross, prayers still flowed out of him. His relationship with God was evident for all to see as three crucial prayers came forth that day. The first was a question: *"my God, my God, why have You forsaken me?"* I believe God answered him by giving him a vision of the church. **Hebrews 12:2** says that *"for the joy set before him he endured the cross."* God deposited within Jesus a picture of the family of God that made sacrificing his life worth it all! Jesus was forsaken by God so we would never be forsaken!

The second prayer of Jesus on the cross was a plea to the Father for forgiveness, not only his actual executors, but for all of humanity: "for they know not what they do." Truthfully, it was the sins of every person who has ever lived that nailed Jesus to the cross, not just that generation's sins. Jesus knew that his sacrifice on behalf of humanity would bring many sons into the Kingdom of his Father. And granting us forgiveness was only possible because of the blood he shed for us. He became sin for us and took its rightful punishment so we could become the righteousness of God and receive the divine life we don't deserve.

The third prayer was a committal of his spirit into the hands of the Father. He knew he had accomplished the Father's will. He had been sent from the Father to redeem fallen humanity and once that was accomplished on the cross it was time to return from where he came. With this revelation he declared, *"It is finished!"* They didn't take his life, he laid it down. These were the last words out of his mouth and then he died. There are some things that we just need to put into the Father's hands. They are outside of our control and we just need to trust Him.

What Would Jesus Do?

From the wilderness to the mountain to the garden and to the cross, Jesus walked in relationship with God continually. Yes, the Spirit of God helped him do what he did, teach what he taught and endure what he endured. But it was because he looked to heaven for help. He got away from the busy-ness of life and ministry to recoup his strength, refresh his spirit and hear what God was speaking to him in each season of his life.

With so much spiritual ministry available to us, it's easy to bypass our true need to connect with the Father directly like Jesus exemplified for us. We can easily convince ourselves that we don't need to spend quality time with the Father because we have received His life through the ministry of others. But this is a trap. Dependency on the ministry of others never produces true spiritual maturity. God wants you to learn to be dependent on the Spirit on a daily basis. What better way to train you for this than spending quality time with the Lord behind closed doors. He wants to help you pray. (**Romans 8:26**)

Look at Jesus' prayer life and its corresponding effects on his relationships and ministry. He didn't force things to happen. He recognized them as they were happening and cooperated with the Father's desire to express His love to others

Other people devote much of their time ministering to others and can fall into another trap: looking for ways to minister to others only to neglect their primary need to receive spiritual life for themselves. When this happens, time that is supposed to be about personal devotions ends up being dominated by the need to build the next sermon for Sunday morning. And prayer time gets consumed with lifting up the needs of others. You get the point. Without putting God first, spiritual life will eventually wane and spiritual burnout will occur. The needs of people will weigh you down because you weren't meant to carry others' burdens to the neglect of your own spirit and the spiritual life of your family.

I would encourage you to dig in a little deeper. Look at Jesus' prayer life and its corresponding effects on his relationships and ministry. He didn't force things to happen. He recognized them as they were happening and cooperated with the Father's desire to express His love to others. That's the grace of God in action! The Holy Spirit's influence in our hearts and in our relationships.

As Jesus said in **Matthew 11:28-30**, *"Come to me, all you who labor and are heavy laden, and I will give you rest. Take my yoke upon you and learn from me, for I am gentle and lowly in heart, and you will find rest for your souls. For my yoke is* *easy and my burden is light."* Religion will wear you out but Jesus will refresh you with the flow of God's Spirit! If there's one thing we need to learn from Jesus, it's how he made prayer a priority and how that prepared his spirit to cooperate with God's Spirit in his life.

CHAPTER TEN

Maximizing Your Personal Prayer Life

*"But you, when you pray, go into your room,
and when you have shut your door, pray to
your Father who is in the secret place; and
your Father you sees in secret will reward
you openly."* **Matthew 6:6**

Make time for intimacy with God. This means you should use good time management to schedule a specific time to spend with the Lord that won't conflict with other responsibilities or be susceptible to distractions. And once you plan to spend time with the Lord, guard that commitment! Be careful that other duties don't crowd out that holy time. Because if you only spend time with God when you don't have anything to do, giving Him your leftovers, you will rarely pray because there's always things vying for our attention!

Some people claim they don't need a set time with the Lord every day because they pray at various times throughout the day. The problem with this can be an issue of intimacy. For example, if you talk with your spouse sporadically throughout the day but don't spend any quality time together, you will miss out on a deeper part of marriage that is available to you.

And if this continues for too long, your marriage could be in jeopardy! The same holds true with your relationship with God. God deserves more than your leftovers and if the truth be told, you need quality time with Him more than you know!

Other people think that if they fulfill their responsibility of a daily prayer time, then they are free to spend the rest of their day doing what they want. But this comes from a religious mindset that gives people a sense of accomplishment because of their good works (prayer), not from a desire to engage in an intimate relationship that involves communication throughout the day. So the prayer box gets checked off the list and off they go pursuing what they want in life instead of staying in constant communication with the One Who abides within. There's a better way.

> *God deserves more than your leftovers and if the truth be told, you need quality time with Him more than you know!*

If Jesus is Lord of your life then He should be Lord over everything, including your time. The Holy Spirit doesn't clock out after you put your time in with God! He abides within you 24 hours a day, ready to interact with you when you are open for His ministry. Just because you fulfill your prayer ritual doesn't mean you can spend the rest of your day pleasing yourself! If you think otherwise this might be a good time to read this Scripture:

> *"Do you not know that your body is a temple of the Holy Spirit, who is in you, whom you*

have received from God? <u>You are not your</u>
<u>own; you were bought at a price.</u> Therefore
honor God with your body."

I Corinthians 6:19, 20

The best scenario would be for us to spend quality time with God (intimacy) on a consistent basis and to touch base with Him throughout each day as our duties allow. OK, I might be in danger of being stoned for saying this, but I would go so far as to say that quality blocks of time aren't necessarily required on a daily basis, but that we should learn to follow the leading of the Spirit in each season of our lives. Quality time with God on a daily basis is definitely the ideal situation but it isn't always realistic with everything going on in our lives. There may be some seasons when you maintain daily devotional time and other seasons when you communicate with God throughout the day and retreat with Him in intervals other than every 24 hours.

Going to the Extreme

Don't become legalistic with measurements of time that God is not bound to. This is for sure, what God may be requiring of you may be altogether different than what He's asking of someone else. So don't judge someone else based on your assignment. And what the Holy Spirit is leading you to do in this season may be different than the last season, or next season for that matter. The key is to follow Holy Spirit's directives for maintaining a strong spirit that communes with Him and cooperates with Him in the spiritual work of prayer.

This is not a license to go weeks on end without making time for God, but it is liberating to get rid of the condemnation that we can feel if we don't measure up to unrealistic expectations we place on ourselves. Or expectations that we allow to loom over us from those who think they know what we should do. Although we are free from condemnation, we should never lose contact with heaven for any reason. We should never allow our flesh or the busyness of life to dictate the activity of our spirit. Take charge of your life by taking care of your spirit.

There are seasons on the mountaintop when revelation seems to be flowing like a river and we can't spend enough time with Him. And there are other times in the valley when life and/or ministry are the focus, times when God expects us to walk out the revelation He has already given us. If your prayer life is static while your life is dynamic, there will be a disconnection between heaven and the affairs of your life. Not that God is willfully withholding anything you need, but when your prayer life is out of sync with that God is saying and doing in your life, the effectiveness of your prayers is greatly diminished.

If you have a genuine relationship with God, you will communicate with Him on a daily basis without being forced to do so by religious obligation. You will talk to Him and listen for His voice because you sincerely love him. A busy schedule can't keep you from communing with God although it can hinder your quality time with Him if you allow it to.

If you have a genuine relationship with God,
you will communicate with Him on a daily basis

*without being forced to do so by religious
obligation*

God is not legalistic. He understands that you have responsibilities that require your attention. He knows you can't always stop what you're doing at the drop of a hat to spend intimate moments with Him. But if you ask the Holy Spirit to help you, He will give you a creative plan to maximize your time so you can spend quality time with the Lord. This may involve multitasking at times or possibly sacrificing sleep, food, entertainment, etc. But if you follow His plan for your time, He will create the opportunity for you to be intimate with Him, because we're all wired for this. We need it desperately! We cannot be fulfilled without it!

If your heart is right with God, you should desire to spend quality time with Him in addition to talking with Him throughout the day. The most important thing is not that you spend hours on end in prayer every day, but that you pay attention to the leading of the Holy Spirit and follow His lead. If you follow through with this, your time with God will be incredibly productive every time you spend time with Him! Quality time cooperating with the Spirit in prayer is far more important than large quantities of time because He knows what is best for us! Your prayer life will be maximized in the Spirit to the degree that you minimize what your flesh cries out for and to the degree that you respond to what your spirit longs for, both of which require the assistance of the Holy Spirit.

Not Competition, It's about Completion

The same principle applies to the Word. You'd be better off reading one verse per day that gets deep inside your spirit, renews your thinking and which you apply to your life, than reading ten chapters per day that don't make a difference in your life. This is not a contest to outperform others or to feel good about your religious efforts to do good Christian things. It is an opportunity to have your heart and life calibrated to the Kingdom of God. It is an invitation to trade your thoughts and ways for His! His are much better!

With so many spiritual tools at our disposal, it is important to use the right one at the right time for the right purpose to accomplish what God desires in your time with Him. For instance, there is a time to pray but there is also a time to worship and yet there's a time for the Word. And in each of these categories there are multiple dimensions you can go into, depending on the direction and timing of the Lord.

This is not a contest to outperform others or to feel good about our religious efforts to do good Christian things. It is an opportunity to have our hearts and lives calibrated to the Kingdom of God

When we insist on using one or two tools all the time, we are bound to become religious in our use of them and eventually lose the results that were intended in the first place. But if we learn to be led by the Holy Spirit each time we connect with Him, we will get results every time! The results are not limited to answered prayers, but include the transformation of our hearts that prepares us to fulfill our Kingdom assignments.

Remember, the Holy Spirit is our Helper. That means that He wants to help us in everything we do, especially in something as important as prayer. He teaches us the Word (**John 14:26**), helps us truly worship God (**John 4:23, 24**) and helps us pray (**Romans 8:26**). **Ephesians 6:18** tells us to pray at all times with all kinds of prayer <u>in the Spirit</u>. This doesn't mean to pray in tongues all the time, although that is a very powerful tool. It means that every time we communicate with God (worship, prayer, Word, etc.) we should rely on the Holy Spirit to lead us in whatever direction He wants to take us. And we know that if we follow His lead then we will get where we need to be in our times with Him.

Also, **Ephesians 6:18** doesn't mean that we should do everything every time we pray! Unfortunately, many believers have been conditioned to pattern their prayer lives after regimented church services they have become accustomed to, most of which contain praise and worship followed by Word and then by prayer every time. Does the Holy Spirit really lead us to sing 3 fast songs and 2 slow songs, do announcements, take up an offering, teach the Word and then do an altar call of some sort Sunday after Sunday? Or are we stuck in the muck of tradition? Just food for thought....

Break Every Tradition!

We are creatures of habit so it's easy to carry on the traditions of those we look to for leadership. We also create our own traditions based on preferences we have in our time with God in prayer. Ultimately, we need to look to the leadership of the Holy Spirit to unravel every tradition that has hindered the effectiveness of our time with God. The

Holy Spirit also wants to develop our capacity to cooperate with Him, using all the spiritual tools at our disposal to develop our spiritual man and to stand in the gap so God's heart can be displayed in our sphere of influence.

And for the record, we don't have to follow a formula based on the 'Lord's prayer.' It was never meant to be recited or to give us a step-by-step pattern for our time with Him. And we definitely don't have to follow a regimented prayer schedule where we pray for the same things every day! We need to be led by the Spirit to get results. It's that simple. Just as Jesus' disciples asked Him to teach them to pray, ask the Holy Spirit the very same thing. He will!

Ultimately, we need to look to the leadership of the Holy Spirit to unravel every tradition that has hindered the effectiveness of our time with God

Praying in tongues is very instrumental to condition your spirit to follow His lead. It strengthens your spirit and sensitizes it to the promptings of the Spirit. This can be helpful if you do it at various times throughout the day, before you spend quality time in prayer and at transitional moments during your prayer time when you don't have a strong leading of the Spirit for your next segment of prayer. Singing in tongues is also instrumental in worship. This can be a catalyst for a new song that He wants to give you or to take you into a greater place of intimacy with God.

There are extremes with everything, both carnal and religious. But God wants us to walk in moderation and be led by the Spirit. That will lead to a productive prayer life that will prepare us for effective living. For example, *"praying without ceasing"* doesn't mean that we should talk to God 24/7. It means that we need a consistent prayer life, to guard the connection we have with the Lord and to pray whenever the need arises. It means we aim to stay in touch with the Lord and allow momentum to continue to build in our spirit. And as soon as we recognize something hindering our connection with the Lord, we deal with it so we don't lose ground.

Some people also become legalistic about the actual time they pray. David did say in the Psalms *"early will I seek Him."* But *"early"* for the NT believer doesn't necessarily mean 5 am or even the first thing you do when you wake up. Prayers don't have a higher success rate in the morning than the evening! It's a matter of priority. The OT principle of 'first fruits' should help us understand that we should give God our best, not what is left over after we've exhausted our resources. So if you are not a morning person, then your 'early' might actually be in the afternoon or evening, when you are awake, alert and at your best. There's nothing worse than trying to pray only to doze off because you're physically exhausted! Find out what works best for you and roll with it!

Seek First the Kingdom

Matthew 6:33 says that we should *"seek first the Kingdom."* This speaks of priority. We should make it a priority to spend quality time with our heavenly Father, positioning ourselves to be aligned to His Kingdom purpose for our lives. Really, what is more important than spending time with the Lord of the Universe? And why wouldn't you want to spend quality time with Him?

There's a train of thought that says if we spend time in prayer, we won't have enough time to take care of our daily responsibilities. But Jesus promised that if we would prioritize His Kingdom above everything else, then He would make sure that everything else would be taken care of. Now before you go scheduling 8 hours of prayer per day, understand that we are also told to "*do all things in moderation.*" We are expected to be good stewards of our finances, relationships and spiritual gifts, all of which involve our time as well. So keep in mind that God doesn't want you to 'rob Peter to pay Paul.' He wants you to live a balanced life.

How you spend your time and money reveals the priorities of your heart. Do yourself a favor: periodically ask the Holy Spirit to adjust your schedule in the same way that you should periodically adjust your financial budget. He will let you know how much time is appropriate for you to spend with your family, pursuing ministry endeavors and in intimacy with Him, which could be different every time you connect with Him. Your personal prayer life is where you should learn how to be led by the Spirit, and making the proper adjustments in your schedule is crucial to staying on track with His leading.

I'd rather pray 15 Spirit-led minutes than 10 hours led by my flesh. Why? Because I'll get results!

Praying 2 hours per day doesn't make you any more spiritual than someone who prays 30 minutes each day. I'd rather pray 15 Spirit-led minutes than 10 hours led by my flesh. Why? Because I'll get results! There are no brownie points in heaven for hours logged in the prayer closet, or Bible chapters read for that matter! Prayer is about getting results in the form of answered prayer, developing spiritual strength, accessing divine wisdom and revelation, cultivating godly character, etc. It's not about putting in your time!

There is tremendous value in disciplining your flesh in obedience to the Spirit, but there is no value in doing things out of tradition or to fulfill religious obligation. We all need the Holy Spirit to lead us each step of the way! If you invest your personal time in intimacy with God, He will invest Himself in your daily walk. If you talk to Him, He will talk to you. If you draw close to Him, He will draw close to you! Take the first step towards greater intimacy with God: make it your ambition to make Him your number one priority and watch God rock your world!

CHAPTER ELEVEN

Read Your Bible

*"But as for you, continue in what you have
learned and have been convinced of, because
you know those from whom you learned it,
and from infancy you have known the Holy
Scriptures, which are able to make you wise
for salvation through faith in Christ Jesus."*
II Timothy 3:14-15

I suppose that a number of people will gloss over this title, simply dismissing what I have to say here because they've been reading the Word for years and therefore don't think they need help in this area. Sadly enough, these same people may very well be the ones that would benefit the most from it! Whether you are picking up the Bible for the first time or have been a student of the Word for decades on end, do yourself a favor and read this with an open mind. You may be in for a pleasant surprise!

Sometimes the church-at-large is guilty of issuing commands without providing the corresponding tools to carry them out successfully. For example, we are constantly told to read our Bibles and witness for Christ and yet very little training is offered to help us do what we're supposed to do. Truthfully, I've attended church services all my life and have never heard (or given) a sermon entitled 'How to Study the Bible.' I believe that church-goers today are told WHAT to believe about the Bible far more than they are taught HOW to discover truth for themselves in the Bible. This really needs to change because according to Ephesians 4:11-16, the main purpose of leadership is to prepare God's people for their ministry to the body of Christ, not to keep them dependent on their ministry.

Church-goers today are told WHAT to believe about the Bible far more than they are taught HOW to discover truth for themselves in the Bible

Of course, it is the responsibility of spiritual parents (five-fold ministry) to teach their children (congregation) what they believe to be true in the Word. But it is also their responsibility to train their children to become mature believers who can hear God's voice, not only through leaders, but also in their own heart through the ministry of the Holy Spirit. Scripture clearly tells us in **John 16:13** that the Holy Spirit is given to every born-again believer to "guide them into all truth." **I John 2:20.27** says it this way: *"...you have an anointing from the Holy One, and <u>all of you</u> know the truth...the anointing you received remains in you, and you do not need anyone to teach you. But just as his anointing teaches you about all things and as that anointing is real, not counterfeit, just as it has taught you, remain in him."*

Now before anyone jumps to the conclusion that we don't need teachers because we can all hear God's voice, let me set

104

something straight. The Apostle John is simply making the point that all believers have a direct connection with the Lord and can recognize truth because of the Holy Spirit's anointing within. He later encourages them in **I John 4:1-6** to put teachers of the Word to the test of authenticity to determine who to listen to and who not to listen to. His exact words were *"do not believe every spirit."* John encouraged them to receive from teachers whose hearts and doctrine were pure, but to reject those whose motivations and teachings were not right.

Discernment Can Protect You

Ultimately, the witness of the Holy Spirit within determines what passes the test, but I believe that a solid understanding of Scripture can aid Him in protecting you from false doctrine. The New Testament is filled with scriptures encouraging the ministry of spiritual leaders and the necessity of every believer to receive from them. But the Bible also advises us to walk in discernment in regards to what others teach because our commitment to follow the Holy Spirit's leading into all truth should be greater than our commitment to believe what a particular minister might teach.

Just because a pastor wears a 3 piece suit and holds a microphone in his hand on Sunday morning doesn't mean that everything that comes out of his mouth is 100% true. Pastors are human too and don't know everything, just like you. So cut them some slack and always look within for the witness of the Spirit to confirm truth to you, which is always in line with the Word of God. While the majority of pastors are undoubtedly truthful in what they speak most of the time,

Scripture is true <u>all</u> of the time. That's why our lives should be built on the foundation of the Word and the witness of the Spirit, not on what someone else has to say.

Do you realize why the Dark Ages were so dark? For starters, the light of the Word wasn't in print form yet and therefore wasn't accessible to the common man. My personal belief is that many spiritual leaders during that time took advantage of this by withholding certain truths from people that would have empowered them to function in their spiritual ministry. Ungodly control replaced a sincere desire to help God's people mature in Christ. The light of God's Word was hidden by the darkness of men's hearts. The Apostle John's exhortation to rely on the anointing within was crucial during this season of Biblical scarcity, but people by-and-large "believed every spirit" instead of following the leading of the Spirit into all truth.

Just because a pastor wears a 3 piece suit and holds a microphone in his hand on Sunday morning doesn't mean that everything that comes out of his mouth is 100% true

What we easily forget is that the Bible wasn't readily available to the church for its first 1500 years! Thank God for the Gutenberg printing press! Thank God for the mass distribution of God's Word worldwide! And thank God for the freedom in this country to read the Word of God and to hear solid Biblical teaching! We are truly privileged to hold the Word of God in our own hands, and yet numbers of believers would rather hear pastors talk about it than hear it from the Author Himself!

There are a number of reasons for this, but I believe that the number one reason lies in the fact that the average Christian just doesn't know <u>how</u> to effectively study God's Word. I've had the privilege of attending Bible schools that are designed to train people for leadership roles in ministry. Part of this training gives guidelines for correct Biblical interpretation. I understand that this is important for those who will consistently minister the Word. But what about those who are encouraged to consistently read and study the Word (which would be all of us)? Why is there an emphasis on one but not the other? Hmmm...

We are All Full-Time Ministers

I'm going to go out on a limb and say that this is because today's church still carries some of the ungodly characteristics that the Dark Ages were known for: a strong clergy/laity separation. Although the Bible is clear that we all are ministers of Christ and even though this truth is commonly voiced from the pulpit, a huge chasm still exists between those who are paid to preach and those who pay for others to preach to them. Statistics tell us that 20% of people in churches today are active participants in the work of the ministry. This is also true regarding financial support for the work of God. These are indicators that church leadership still has room for improvement in terms of empowering people to become everything God has called them to be.

Although the vast majority of believers aren't called to be theologians, we can all study the Word effectively with a little training. If Christians aren't taught how to discover truth in God's Word firsthand, reading the Bible will only serve the purpose of furthering the indoctrination they receive from the pulpit. Before you pick up a stone to throw at me, allow me to explain.

> *If Christians aren't taught how to discover truth in God's Word firsthand, reading the Bible will only serve the purpose of furthering the indoctrination they receive from the pulpit*

It is very common for ministers of the Word to insert their slant on scripture into their sermons, which is then downloaded into the minds of their parishioners. They are simply telling it like they see it. But this can be dangerous, especially when it is served on a 'believe it because I said so' platter. People often respond to these types of messages by reading between the lines of their Bibles only to hear the voice of their pastor instead of the Holy Spirit. In this way, beliefs are easily engraved on their minds which then become roadblocks to truths being birthed in their spirits.

Interestingly enough, the first century church seemed to have great spiritual success despite not having the written Word to fall back on. Even if the Bible we have today was around then it wouldn't have mattered all that much due to the fact that the vast majority of people back then were illiterate. In fact, the church leaders of that time didn't even have the New Testament to guide them in their ministry. But they all had the Holy Spirit within, who used the Old Testament scriptures in the form of individual scrolls to reassure their beliefs and practices in light of the age of grace. So why should we study the New Testament in light of the fact that the first century church did just fine without it? That's a great question worth exploring.

The Word of God is Progressive

The New Testament we have today as a part of our Bible is a result of the first century believers living out their faith based on the leadership of the Holy Spirit in their midst. And they did this by studying their Bible, which consisted of the Old Testament, and by receiving inspiration from the Holy Spirit to apply it to their lives. The New Testament is actually filled with quotes from the Old Testament that the Spirit made to come alive in their hearts. Their everyday lives were very much shaped by the same Word their predecessors heard from God.

In similar fashion, our sermons and songs today are filled with quotes from the New Testament that have been breathed on in our hearts by the Holy Spirit. We're blessed today by the ministry of the first century church because it's all the same living, breathing Word of God that continues to unfold an ever-increasing revelation of God Almighty! Because the Word of God is living, it spans numerous generations to bring life and illumination to those who will receive it through the ministry of the Holy Spirit. Amazing, isn't it? God's Word connects His people from the beginning to the end of time! If we want to know God for ourselves then it would be wise for us to connect with those who have known Him in previous generations (through the Word) as well as those who know Him today (through spiritual relationships in the church).

Like the early church, our spiritual success is also dependent upon the leadership of the Holy Spirit, who uses both the Old and New Testaments to establish His truth in our lives today. Because the Word of God is alive, we can be encouraged by it even though it was originally spoken to people who lived hundreds of years ago! The truth is that God's Word is progressive in its revelation of who God is. Studying the Word gives us access into the dynamics of the Spirit in the lives of other people, including what God spoke to them, their response to His voice and how that revolutionized their lives. By recognizing the voice of God in previous generations, we can gain a greater awareness of what God is saying to us right now! All because the Word is alive!

Because the Word of God is living, it spans numerous generations to bring life and illumination to those who will receive it through the ministry of the Holy Spirit

What separates the Bible from every other book on the planet is the fact that it is divinely inspired and has been orchestrated to form a cohesive collection of books (66 to be exact) that detail God speaking to various people from various walks of life on various continents during various periods of time. From beginning to end, we have a progressive revelation of who God is and what that means to us today. With 40 different authors who lived in different cultures in very different circumstances, only one thing remains constant: the never-changing purpose of God revealed through His Word to each one of us!

Allow me to encourage you to not only read and study the Word, but take the time to invest in your ability to understand it. Of course, listen to messages by your pastor and other spiritual leadership. But also seek out those who can personally mentor you with principles of the Word. And pursue some basic training in biblical interpretation. Acquire some study tools that will aid you in understanding some basic Greek and Hebrew, biblical culture in the time Scripture was written, as well as the context each book of the Bible took place in. A little understanding goes a long way in knowing how to apply the Word to your life! It can protect you from assuming things that aren't true and can pave the way for you to gain revelation that you've never known!!

Your relationship with the Word is an adventure and should be exciting, not boring! You need to welcome the Holy Spirit as your instructor as well as do your due diligence to equip yourself to explore the depths of wisdom within the pages of Scripture. Just make it your aim to know the God of the Word, not just the Word of God!! And God will reveal Himself to you through His Word more each day!

CHAPTER TWELVE

Explore Your Options in God

"Take the helmet of salvation and the sword of the Spirit, which is the word of God. And pray in the Spirit on all occasions with all kinds of prayers and requests."

Ephesians 6:17-18

We are creatures of habit. Chances are most of you reading this sit in the same general section, if not the exact seats, every time you attend church. Am I right? Granted, some people fly by the seat of their pants more than others, but we all have certain ways of doing things without thinking much about it. Like taking care of personal hygiene, getting ready for bed or exercise routines (or a lack thereof).

This holds true for our relationship with God and what transpires during the time we spend with Him. Depending on the church culture that is responsible for shaping our perspective of God and our communication with Him, we all have varying spiritual habits that comprise our time with God. Some people are more inclined to abide by these habits than others, but we all have the tendency to gravitate towards certain values that were presented to us early in our Christian life.

---

*The Word encourages us to welcome the
ministry of the Spirit to assist us in
communicating with God on multiple levels*

What I am about to list are options that I would encourage you to explore in God. Allow me to explain. Certain groups in the body of Christ instill the importance of Bible reading to the people in their reach, whereas other groups stress the necessity of spending quality time in daily prayer. And yet others emphasize private worship, praying in tongues or the confession of the Word, and the list goes on and on. Point is, there are varying priorities that are laid out in different denominations and churches that motivate people to communicate with God in a specific way. Maybe it's time to explore some additional options!

I think we would all agree that prayer and Bible reading are both important for believers to engage in consistently. But we may not agree with the amount of time we should spend in prayer or the amount of Bible verses we should read every day. Truthfully, there is no clear-cut formula laid out in the Word for us to follow, so there is room for private interpretation and application here. What we do know is that the Word encourages us to welcome the ministry of the Spirit to assist us in communicating with God on multiple levels.

"But the Counselor, the Holy Spirit, whom the Father will send in my name, will teach you all things and will remind you of everything I have said to you." **John 14:2**

"In the same way, the Spirit helps us in our weakness. We do not know what we ought to pray for, but the Spirit Himself intercedes for us with groans that words cannot express." **Romans 8:26**

"I urge, then, first of all, that requests, prayers, intercession and thanksgiving be made for everyone." **I Timothy 2:1**

"The prayer of a righteous man is powerful and effective." **James 5:16**

After reading these Scriptures, you can easily conclude that there are a variety of types of communication with God and that the Spirit wants to help us function effectively in them. It's also apparent that if we want a powerful, effective prayer life then we need to receive the empowerment of the Spirit to achieve it, not by self-righteous works, but by receiving and responding to the grace He supplies.

I'm going to break our communication with God into 3 categories (prayer, word, & worship) and then proceed to list a number of sub-categories that pertain to these areas. I will also give a brief description of each area that presents an opportunity to commune with God. It's up to you to explore these avenues of communication with God. And allow me to highly recommend the Holy Spirit as your personal navigator! Take God out of the box of your religious upbringing. Not that it's bad, just probably incomplete. There's more to God than any of us know at this very moment, so let's explore our options in Him!

PRAYER

1. **Petitions** – asking God to do something for you or in you, or to give something to you
2. **Intercessions** – praying for the needs of others or situations outside your control
3. **Questions** – asking God questions
4. **Sharing Burdens** – expressing your feelings, thoughts and desires to the Lord
5. **Silence** – listening for the voice of God within
6. **Submission** – surrendering your desires to God so He can reshape them according to His will
7. **Tongues/Interpretations** – praying in unknown languages as the Spirit gives you the ability to do so, as well as the interpretation of mysteries that are spoken by the Spirit through you
8. **Warfare** - putting a stop to the work of demons and liberating the ministry of angels in your life

WORD

1. **Reading the Word** – verse by verse, chapter by chapter reading of various books of the Bible

2. **Studying the Word** – a much slower pace than reading, paying attention to details and investigating original languages of Scripture, culture and history behind Scripture, etc.

   a. **Topical studies** – focusing on a particular theme throughout the Bible

   b. **Book studies** – focusing on a particular book of the Bible

   c. **Character studies** – focusing on a particular person in the Bible

   d. **Word studies** – focusing on particular words or phrases that are repeated in the Bible

3. **Meditating on the Word** – thinking deeply about words, phrases, sentences, paragraphs and sections of Scripture in order to gain deeper meaning than what is on the surface

4. **Memorizing the Word** – committing various Scripture verses to memory

5. **Confessing the Word** – speaking the Word out loud to activate your faith in God's Word and to renew your mind with God's thoughts

6. **Prophesying the Word** – speaking God's promises over your life and others

WORSHIP

1. **Thanksgiving** – giving God thanks for what He has done and for what He has given you

2. **Praise** – giving God credit for His good deeds, speaking well of Him

3. **Worship** – expressing to God how much he is worth to you, loving Him because of Who He is

As you can see from the list of options above, there are many different directions your time with God can go. That's why it's important to ask the Holy Spirit to lead you, teaching you how to pray just like Jesus did for his disciples. Believe it or not, whether your prayer life is effective or not depends on if you allow the ministry of the Holy Spirit to be active in your heart and life. *Personal devotions* aren't just about asking God for stuff and reading a cool Book. They are <u>the pursuit of man after the heart of God while depending on the Spirit to help us pray as well as understand and apply a book that He inspired in the first place!</u>

For those of you who have read the Bible but have never studied it, get ready for a spirit of revelation and wisdom to hit you, bringing the Word alive in your heart and generating faith for God to impact your life with the gems you discover by digging a little deeper! For those who always talk in prayer but never listen for His voice, get ready to discover that prayer is a two-way street! God is going to train you to discern the difference between His thoughts and yours. You get the picture. When you step out of your comfort zone and explore your options in your time with Him, there's no limit to what God can do for you, in you and through you!

It's important for you to receive ministry from others so you can receive an impartation of the grace in their lives that makes certain things easy

---

I will say that it's normal to have certain preferences based on your God-given gifts. For instance, if God has graced you with a teaching gift your hunger will most likely lead you to read and study the Word more often than others. Or if you've been blessed with prophetic grace you will most likely find it easier to pray than others. But this is not an excuse to neglect other ways God has endorsed to build your relationship with Him! That's why it's important for you to receive ministry from others so you can receive an impartation of the grace in their lives that makes certain things easy. This will make you more balanced and ultimately brings maturity to your life.

For this reason, it's impossible to totally separate your personal relationship with Christ from your connection to His body. Because God has invested Himself in His church, you need to have relationships with other believers so you can discover the greatness of God within their lives. We actually get to know God more by getting to know people more and receiving what God has put inside them! Amazing, isn't it?

Conclusion

Regardless of the magnitude of your revelation, you still need grace to walk it out. And your personal prayer life has a lot to do with accessing that grace. Yes, *"faith gives you access to grace,"* but faith needs the context of an active relationship with God to be birthed and developed to the point of fruition. "Faith comes by hearing the word of God," so you need to position yourself to hear His voice by pursuing the Lord on a consistent basis. And once faith is birthed in your heart, what you do with that faith is crucial to the growth and ultimately, the fulfillment of God's Word in your life.

You can exercise your faith in the direction of your choosing, provided it is in line with His Word. And grace will be released in proportion to your faith. But if you want to experience the *"abundance of grace,"* then your faith needs to be coordinated with your part in God's Kingdom, not just your personal needs. It's the difference between the Israelites who experienced supernatural provision and protection in the wilderness and those who actually entered the Promised Land to access their inheritance in the Lord. I don't know about you, but I want to access everything God has in store for me, but most of all, I want my life to serve God's Kingdom purpose in the lives of others!

A prayer life that is led by the Holy Spirit is the entrance through which God's Kingdom expands in your heart and life

Too often we settle for less than what God has provided for us, becoming comfortable with the status quo. We become satisfied with our spiritual experiences in the past and look at yesterday as the 'good old days.' But I declare to you that your best days are ahead of you! The best is yet to come! If you will invite the presence and Person of the Holy Spirit to saturate your prayer life with heaven's intention, you will never be the same. You will crave to be in His presence! You will long to hear His voice and communicate with Him. You will discover that having an ongoing conversation with the Father is not burdensome, it is the ultimate joy in life!

A prayer life that is led by the Holy Spirit is always an adventure that never disappoints! He will take you places you've never been and will do things in and through you that you never dreamed possible! It is the entrance through which God's Kingdom expands in your heart and life. *"Let Your Kingdom come! Let Your will be done on earth as it is in heaven!!"* This is the heart cry of those who allow the Holy Spirit to do what He was sent to do: help us cooperate with heaven in our lives. Holy Spirit, teach us to pray effectively just as Jesus taught his disciples. Help us see Kingdom perspective that includes our personal needs, but more importantly focuses on the heart of the King! We are yours God, have Your way!

APPENDIX ONE

A Quick Guide to a Balanced Christian Life

"They devoted themselves to the apostles'
teaching and to the fellowship, to the
breaking of bread and to prayer." **Acts 2:42**

1. Consistent, Spirit-Led Communication with God
    (<u>Personal Devotions</u>)
    a. Prayer
    b. Word
    c. Worship
2. <u>Ongoing Conversations</u> with God throughout each
    Day
    a. Quiet Prayer
    b. Meditation
    c. Thanksgiving, Praise & Worship
    d. Praying in Tongues
3. Spontaneous Seasons of God-Focused Time
    (<u>Occasional Retreats</u> with God)
4. Gathering Regularly with <u>the Local Church</u>
    a. Praising & Worshiping God
    b. Giving Financially
    c. Receiving the Word through Your Leadership

    d. Receiving Prayer and Ministry from Your Leadership

    e. Ministering One to Another

5. <u>Receiving Discipleship</u> through Personal Relationships

6. <u>Sharing Fellowship</u> through Personal Relationships

7. <u>Mentoring</u> others through Personal Relationships

8. <u>Evangelizing</u> others through Personal Relationships

9. <u>Reaching Out</u> to Believers who Can't Make it to Church Gatherings

10. Engaging in <u>Missions</u> (Pray, Give and/or Go)

11. Participating in <u>Community-Life Meetings</u> or Smalls Groups (I Corinthians 14:26)

12. Receiving Ministry through <u>Guest Ministers</u> (Local Church or Special Meetings)

13. Receiving Ministry through <u>Second-Hand Resources</u> (TV, Radio, Books, Blogs, Teaching CD's/DVD's, Internet coverage of live meetings, etc.)

14. <u>Giving</u> to those who are Less Fortunate than You

15. <u>Ministering</u> to those God puts in your Path

16. <u>Interceding</u> for those God puts on your Heart

It is my personal conviction that these items aren't optional. We can't treat them like a buffet, picking what we like and walking right by what we don't like. Every single item listed above is substantiated by scripture, not for a select few, but for every believer. If you want to grow in Christ and become more useful in His hands, prayerfully look over this list and ask God to show you what you may have neglected. Don't walk in condemnation over what you're not doing; be enlightened to what you have the opportunity to do in your Christian journey. Fully engage yourself in the Christian life and see what God can do both in and through you!

Don't walk in condemnation over what you're not doing, be enlightened to what you have the opportunity to do

---

APPENDIX TWO

Devotional Log

Month _____

Keep in mind, there are no right or wrong answers here. If you are honest with God, yourself and those you choose to share this information with, this devotional log will serve as a tool to help you track and develop your relationship with God. These questions outline various ways that God wants to speak to you as well as your responsibility to allow His Word to influence your life. Reviewing your answers from time to time will give you a sense of God's progressive work in your life and will equip you to minister to others what God has ministered to you.

What are you believing God for in prayer?

What prayers have been answered recently?

What has God spoken to you about personally?

What has God taught you through your spiritual leadership?

What has God spoken to you as a result of your spiritual relationships outside of church services?

What Bible passages or spiritual books have you been reading?

What special church services or ministry media (TV, Radio, teaching CD's) have you been blessed by?

What truths have you discovered through these spiritual resources (Bible passages, books, special services & ministry media)?

How have you applied what you have learned in your life?

How has God changed your life recently (character, thought life, decisions, relationships)?

What role has personal praise and worship had in your relationship with God?

What has been the emphasis in your devotional life recently (personal prayer, intercession for others, Bible reading, Bible study, worship, meditation)?

What unique ways has the Holy Spirit lead you in your prayer life and in praying for others?

Biography

Bo Salisbury has ministered the Word of God for over 27 years throughout the US and around the world. Through *Kingdom Culture International* he has ministered in 34 nations in churches, leadership conferences, Bible colleges, prisons, open air crusades, prophetic training workshops and other seminars.

His apostolic teaching and prophetic preaching strengthens churches and encourages leaders to break through every barrier standing in the way of Kingdom expansion in their lives, relationships, ministries and territories. He is passionate about revival, reform and unity in the body of Christ and his ministry is characterized by signs and wonders. He is also an author, songwriter and leads a ministerial network called *Kingdom Culture Exchange* consisting of leaders throughout the US and around the world. He also leads *Kingdom Culture Institute*, an online school of ministry for up-and-coming leaders and existing church leaders who desire to upgrade their understanding of Kingdom Culture.

Kingdom Culture Institute

Kingdom Culture Institute takes 30 years of combined Bible School and ministry experience and makes it accessible through biblical, practical, relational and revelatory teaching. This online school of ministry is designed to lay biblical foundation in those who feel called into ministry, for leaders in ministry who never had any systematic ministry training and for experienced leaders who are updating their ministry wineskin to be congruent with Kingdom culture.

It is also beneficial for elders and ministry workers in local churches who want to improve their spiritual understanding and effectiveness in ministry. Senior leaders may want their staff and lay leaders to take these classes to improve productivity. The advantages of this (**KCI**) as opposed to sending them off to a Bible college is continued relationship, ministry involvement in the local church and financial support remaining in the senior pastor's church instead of somewhere else.

In addition to teaching, this online school will feature time for Q&A at the end of every class, references for additional study material (Scripture and books) for those hungry to learn more on their own and homework assignments/tests. This will not be a strictly academic environment as much of the material wasn't learned in a classroom but in real life ministry experience. So in addition to biblical knowledge there will be plenty of wisdom imparted to prepare others in ways formal training doesn't normally address. Plus there will be occasional prophetic ministry, prayer, etc.

Classes will be Mondays and Tuesdays from 7-8:30 pm EST. All classes will be archived so students can access them later if their schedule doesn't allow them to be in the live class or if they simply want to reinforce what was learned previously. Those watching the archived classes can still submit questions that will be answered at the beginning of the next class.

KCI is divided into 4 categories with 8 classes pertaining to each category, also with a spring and fall semester. Each semester maintains the 4 categories but with totally different classes. And there are special summer courses as well.

Kingdom Culture Exchange

Kingdom Culture Exchange is made up of leaders who have connected in spirit and have committed to walk together toward divine purpose. The concepts of apostolic networks and ministerial alliances have been around for decades, impressing on us the need to align vertically with apostolic covering and horizontally with spiritual fellowship. **Kingdom Culture Exchange** incorporates both concepts and additionally places great emphasis on the need to function as the spiritual family that we are.

When Jesus laid the foundation for the church within the context of his closest disciples, a community began to develop consisting of disciples who related to Jesus, AND to one another. A spiritual family began to emerge as Jesus shifted their paradigm concerning leadership and ministry away from the influence of the culture around them, to Kingdom culture. He presented the idea of leadership as servanthood, as opposed to what they saw in those who ruled natural organizations.

Jesus emphatically said to them in **Matthew 20:25-27**, *"...the rulers of the Gentiles lord it over them, and those who are great exercise authority over them. Yet IT SHALL NOT BE SO AMONG YOU; whoever desires to become great among*

135

you, let him be your servant. And whoever desires to be first among you, let him be your slave." The disciples of Jesus desired to rule in the context of Roman dominance. They weren't thinking of serving in the context of family, the most prominent metaphor for church in the NT.

In local church gatherings, regional Kingdom activity and national/international networking, there is a great need to function like the family of God that Jesus envisioned, not like businesses, politics or entertainment. Gatherings of believers, and networks of leaders for that matter, cannot be facilitated like earthly institutions and be expected to obtain heavenly results.

Organization is necessary to facilitate what God organically initiates, but I'm convinced we have all-too-often gotten the cart ahead of the horse in many spiritual organizations today including local churches, ministerial alliances, denominations and apostolic networks.

Kingdom Culture Exchange exists to facilitate Kingdom activity through the power of relationships, allowing God to initiate, develop and transition relationships according to His desire. This is not a one-size-fits all organization. It allows for various types of relationships and ministry that flows forth out of them. It is a safe, refreshing place to connect and cooperate as the family of God.

Whether you're in full-time ministry, are bi-vocational or are a marketplace minister, **Kingdom Culture Exchange** is designed to enhance who you are as an individual, develop you as a minister and increase the effectiveness of your ministry.

For more information visit the website at:
https://kingdomculture.life/kingdom-culture-exchange/

Kingdom Culture Media

To see all the *Teaching Cd's, Books and Prophetic Instrumentals* available to enrich your spiritual life, please visit us at: https://kingdomculture.life/store OR request a Product Catalog to be emailed/mailed to you

Contact Info

To contact Bo Salisbury regarding speaking engagements, *Grace Life Consultation* or *Grace Life Oasis*, please visit the ministry website at: http://kingdomculture.life OR

Email us at: bo@kingdomculture.life OR

Mail us at: **PO Box 2315 North Canton, OH 44720**

Facebook.com/bosalisbury72
Instagram.com/Bosalisbury72/

Donations to Kingdom Culture International

If you want to donate to support world missions, leadership development and the establishment of churches, you can do so online at the website above, the mailing address above or at: **palpal.me/BoSalisbury**

Made in the USA
Monee, IL
15 July 2020